D0761619

**NEW DIRECTIONS
FOR TESTING
AND MEASUREMENT**

Number 8 • 1980

NEW DIRECTIONS FOR TESTING AND MEASUREMENT

A Quarterly Sourcebook
William B. Schrader, Editor-in-Chief

Number 8, 1980

Measurement Aspects of Title I Evaluations

Gary Echternacht
Guest Editor

Jossey-Bass Inc., Publishers
San Francisco • Washington • London

MEASUREMENT ASPECTS OF TITLE I EVALUATIONS
New Directions for Testing and Measurement
Number 8, 1980
      Gary Echternacht, Guest Editor

New Directions for Testing and Measurement is published
quarterly by Jossey-Bass Inc., Publishers. Subscriptions are
available at the regular rate for institutions, libraries, and
agencies of $30 for one year. Individuals may subscribe at the
special professional rate of $18 for one year.

Correspondence:
Subscriptions, single-issue orders, change of address notices,
undelivered copies, and other correspondence should be sent to
New Directions Subscriptions, Jossey-Bass Inc., Publishers,
433 California Street, San Francisco, California 94104.

Editorial correspondence should be sent to the Editor-in-Chief,
William B. Schrader, ETS, Princeton, New Jersey 08541.

Library of Congress Catalogue Card Number LC 80-84308
International Standard Serial Number ISSN 0271-0609
International Standard Book Number ISBN 87589-870-X

Cover design by Willi Baum
Manufactured in the United States of America

Contents

Editor's Notes   Gary Echternacht   vii

Title I Evaluation and Reporting System: Gary Echternacht   1
Development of Evaluation Models

    The federally mandated evaluation system is the result of past failures to
provide Congress with accurate information on the Title I program.
This chapter describes the background leading to the evaluation models.

Internal Validity of the ESEA Title I   Steve Murray   17
Evaluation Models   Judy Arter

    Internal validity is rarely considered by users of the evaluation models.
This chapter outlines threats to internal validity posed by the evaluation
models.

Toward Functional Criteria for   Kenneth M. Wilson   33
Functional-Level Testing in   Thomas F. Donlon
Title I Evaluation

    Although functional-level testing is fundamental to each of the evalua-
tion models, its meaning has remained unclear. In this chapter criteria
for functional-level testing are proposed.

Discussion: Assessing the Reliability and   Bruce L. Stewart   51
Validity of Chance-Level Scores

    Two of the three methods Wilson and Donlon suggest for evaluation are
based on an inappropriate model of examinee behavior.

Discussion: Toward Functional Criteria for   Paul Raffeld   55
Functional-Level Testing in
Title I Evaluation

    Wilson and Donlon's chapter views out-of-level testing from the limited
perspective of a student taking the test. Motivational effects must be
considered.

Regression Toward the Mean and the   A. O. H. Roberts   59
Regression-Effect Bias

    Regression effects in the evaluation models have been hotly debated.
This chapter discusses the extent to which the regression effect can be
controlled.

Discussion: Regression Toward the Mean   Robert L. Linn   83
and the Interval Between
Test Administrations

    If the correlation between selection test and pretest is greater than the
correlation between selection test and posttest, a selected group will continue to regress to the mean in the norm-referenced model.

vi

Discussion: Underlying Assumptions and   Robert S. Burton   91
Resulting Biases

In Roberts' chapter the regression effect was discussed using a two-variable model while the norm-referenced model relies on three test administrations.

Index   97

Editor's Notes

To see that ESEA Title I evaluation is a popular topic among professional evaluators, one only needs to thumb through any of the annual AERA/NCME meeting programs since 1977. Papers are being presented by supporters and critics alike. Methodology, policy, and utilization are the subjects of most papers.

The acronym ESEA stands for the Elementary and Secondary Education Act, a compensatory education program begun in 1965 as part of President Johnson's Great Society. Title I of that Act was aimed at providing local school districts with funds for compensatory education programs. ESEA Title I was the first federal education legislation to require program evaluation. It is also the largest federal education program at the elementary and secondary level. As such, we find that Title I evaluation accounts for more "evaluation work" than any other educational program.

Title I evaluation's poor record of performance has been well documented. Two different approaches have been used to evaluate the program. One approach has relied on a system of collecting and synthesizing locally developed evaluations. Each school district must perform an evaluation of its Title I program. These evaluations are reported to the state where they are summarized into a state report. State reports are then summarized into a national report by the federal government. The second approach has been to commission national studies. Both approaches have yielded disappointing results. Locally developed evaluations have suffered from a lack of comparability in design and poor quality in the data collected. National evaluations have fared no better. Poor quality data and methodological problems have reduced their effectiveness.

In reaction to this poor record for program evaluation, Congress passed legislation in 1974 directing future Title I evaluations. Pulling together locally designed evaluations was preferred to conducting national evaluations because local evaluations were believed to result in better local programs. To overcome problems of poor quality data, local districts were required to abide by certain technical standards. To overcome problems of noncomparability, local districts were required to use specific evaluation models. This standardized approach made it easier to pull together evaluation results. The consequence of this legislation is the Title I Evaluation and Reporting System (TIERS).

TIERS uses a summative approach. Each evaluation model attempts to estimate the extent to which Title I students grow in achievement as a consequence of Title I. The evaluation models are the core of a good evaluation design, not the complete design. Formative evaluation is encouraged, but it is not reported to higher levels.

Many people have been involved in the development of TIERS. RMC Corporation, Mountain View, California, was responsible for the initial development, and they remain actively involved in refining the system. Both

Oscar Roberts and Bruce Stewart, who contributed to this issue, have been key RMC staff working on TIERS. Since 1976 regional technical assistance centers have been assisting states and local school districts in the use of evaluation models. Steve Murray, Judy Arter, Kenneth Wilson, Paul Raffeld, and Robert Burton have worked on the technical assistance project. Finally, while Robert Linn and Tom Donlon have not worked directly with TIERS, both have contributed to its development.

The chapters in this volume represent an inside view of Title I evaluation. Six of the ten authors are or have been on the staffs of the regional technical assistance centers. Two authors are RMC staff responsible for developing and refining TIERS.

In this volume, I provide a context for Title I evaluation by outlining its history and the general issues that have been raised. Steve Murray and Judy Arter look at issues surrounding the internal validity of the TIERS evaluation models. Both of these are general chapters. Their purposes are to raise questions and to outline structures for discussion.

The last two papers in the issue deal with specific aspects of the evaluation models. Each of these papers presents a point of view about testing and evaluation. In Kenneth Wilson and Thomas Donlon's chapter, the notion of functional level testing is discussed — both in its meaning and application. The notion of functional level testing is fundamental to TIERS, as most Title I students have below average achievement levels. Paul Raffeld and Bruce Stewart discuss the chapter. In the final chapter, Oscar Roberts discusses the regression effect as it applies to the model that most school districts use. Perhaps the most widely discussed aspect of TIERS is the extent to which the regression occurs. This point has always been hotly debated. The debate continues in this issue in the discussion by Robert Burton and Robert Linn.

Although this issue is titled *Measurement Aspects of Title I Evaluation* and the chapters are about TIERS specifically, careful attention will show that the problems and issues raised are not unique to TIERS. They are characteristic of all summative educational evaluations employing achievement tests. There can be no question that TIERS represents an enormous improvement in the way local evaluations are used at the federal level. The remaining questions are the degree of accuracy in the results reported to Congress and the extent to which these results satisfy the needs of Congress in funding decisions and making general policy.

Gary Echternacht
Guest Editor

Gary Echternacht is director of the Region II ESEA Title I Technical Assistance Center for the Educational Testing Service, Princeton, New Jersey.

The federally mandated evaluation system resulted from
past failures to provide Congress with accurate
information on how well Title I was working.
The new system is designed to aggregate
locally developed evaluations into a
national summary.

Title I Evaluation and Reporting System: Development of Evaluation Models

Gary Echternacht

The Elementary and Secondary Education Act (ESEA) of 1965 was the first federal social legislation to require periodic program evaluation. Section 124(g) of Title I states that a school district may receive funds only if "effective procedures are adopted for evaluating . . . the effectiveness of the programs assisted under this title in meeting the special educational needs of educationally deprived children." The impetus behind this requirement came from Senator Robert Kennedy, whose motive seems to have been to give children and their parents a way of knowing if the programs were working (see, for example, Hendrickson, 1978; McLaughlin, 1975). That same legislation also had a reporting requirement, which was strengthened by the 1967 amendments requiring that the Department of Health, Education and Welfare annually provide Congress with "a report evaluating the results and effectiveness of programs and projects assisted thereunder" (McLaughlin, 1975).

As Hendrickson (1978) points out, the legislation pertaining to evaluation had two distinct purposes. On the one hand, program evaluation was to provide accountability at the local level. On the other hand, program evaluation was to provide Congress with a national picture of how well Title I was working. Although not mutually exclusive, the implications of these aims often run counter to each other in terms of design, measurement, and conduct of the evaluation. For example, in designing a national evaluation of Title I it would be necessary to standardize criteria, measures, and design so that data from different sites could be combined into a coherent set. Yet such standardization works against local accountability. General Title I program objectives and procedures may be set by the federal government, but curricula are specified by local districts. Tests and designs appropriate for judging one program are often inappropriate for judging other programs.

Title I Evaluation 1965-1976

From the beginning, school people have distrusted program evaluation. Some have seen program evaluation as an example of federal intrusion into education. More frequently, school people have feared the comparisons that might be made among teachers, schools, and school districts. These forces have been in place since program evaluation came into being and are an integral part of the politics of evaluation. They have also hampered the progress of good program evaluation because evaluators must deal with political realities. Thus, evaluation practice has been slow to evolve.

Before ESEA there were no people in school districts who were responsible for what we would call program evaluation today. Before 1965 evaluation consisted of "asking teachers whether the children were reading better" (Hendrickson, 1978). The evaluation experts of the time resided primarily in universities and colleges. Their tools were classical experimental designs, randomization, and laboratory control. They did not know how schools worked, how Title I programs were actually designed, or the political context in which programs were set. People who became evaluators at the local level as a result of ESEA were either teachers or administrators, possibly having some experience with standardized testing, and having little or no training in statistical methodology.

Thus, the earliest Title I evaluations were of low quality. The federal Title I Office, which administered the program nationally, was charged with the responsibility of reporting to Congress on the effect of Title I. Their approach was to rely on the evaluation reports which were prepared for local accountability. These local reports were sent to the state education department where the state synthesized them into a state report, which, in turn was sent to the federal Title I Office. These state reports were synthesized into a national report to Congress. Nevertheless, the problems were manifold. Initially, the federal government provided little direction to states and local districts on how to assemble the data they collected. The consequence was an unmanageable situation where reports were not comparable and little information could be conveyed in the national report. Attempts to standardize this process to introduce more comparability failed. Instructions were lengthy and complex, and the quality of the data submitted remained poor.

The Office of the Assistant Secretary for Planning and Evaluation became concerned about the poor quality of data in the state reports and set out to do a national study of Title I. Data from 132 schools in eleven districts that were believed to be exemplary were collected to determine the effects of the program and to relate those effects to the costs. The study, commonly called the TEMPO study, produced negative results. No evidence of improved reading achievement was found. Criticism of the study was widespread, but the study did have an effect. Much too much has been expected of Title I. Hopes for enormous gains were dashed, although the program retained widespread support.

In 1968 responsibility for preparing a national Title I report was moved from the Title I Office to the Bureau of Elementary and Secondary Education. The general approach was also changed. State reports were no longer used. States were still required to submit annual reports, but their scope was reduced. Unlike past years where the Title I Office prepared only its report to Congress, this bureau assumed responsibility for evaluating all titled programs under ESEA. A national report was to be developed based on national surveys of local school districts. These surveys came to be part of a massive federal data collection system called Belmont, which collected data on fifteen other federal programs in addition to Title I. As in the TEMPO study, the surveys relied on locally collected data. Whatever pre- and postachievement data was available was reported for grades two, four, and six. Improving on the TEMPO design, more schools and districts were included in the design.

Nevertheless, the quality of the achievement data collected locally remained low. Much was not reported, much was inappropriate, and much was obviously in error. The data were not comparable from district to district. Procedures and metrics used to indicate achievement differed, again making it difficult to compile a concise report to Congress on the effect of Title I.

The findings from these surveys were generally negative. Title I students gained less than the students with whom they were compared. Program reviews conducted at about this time (Washington Research Project, 1969) began to explain some of the negative findings: many programs failed to follow federal guidelines and program criteria, many nonacademic services were funded, and much service was provided to children without a critical need for compensatory services (Wargo and others, 1972).

In 1970 the federal responsibility for evaluation again changed. The Office of Planning, Budgeting, and Evaluation (OPBE), now the Office of Program Evaluation, assumed control over Title I evaluation. Approaches changed too. State evaluative reports remained the responsibility of the Title I Office, where they were used in managing the program. The Title I Office needed these state reports but lacked the authority to standardize them. In response to its new charge, OPBE began a series of studies reviewing past state and local evaluation reports.

Three studies were conducted, each covering a different time span. The first report, covering 1965 through 1970, was prepared by the American Institutes for Research (Wargo and others, 1972); the second, covering 1971 through 1974, was prepared by RMC Corporation (Gamel, Tallmadge, Wood, and Binkley, 1975); and the third, covering 1969 through 1974, was prepared by Stanford Research Institute (Thomas and Pelavin, 1976). Although these three studies differed considerably, there is a common thread running through them. Each cites poor quality data, noncomparability of approach, and reliance on a grade-equivalent standard as limiting factors in the study.

OPBE's major emphasis was on performing an independent national study. This was performed by Educational Testing Service (ETS). Their effort was the most systematic and controlled yet. It used a random sample and control groups. The analyses were extremely complex and voluminous. In general they showed a small positive effect for the program.

Before the ETS study was completed, however, Congress had become frustrated over the progress that had been made in evaluating ESEA Title I. As an outgrowth of this frustration, when ESEA was extended in 1974, the basic evaluation requirements were changed. Much more directive than before, they required the following:

1. Independent evaluations measuring the impact of the program.
2. Development of standards for evaluations and a schedule to ensure evaluating a representative sample of programs each year.
3. Development of evaluation models that would produce comparable data.
4. Technical assistance to help states and local districts apply the standards and models.

In June 1974, RMC Corporation was awarded a contract to begin development of the evaluation models and accompanying reporting system. Prototypes were developed and reviewed extensively by states and local districts (Bessey, Rosen, Chiang, and Tallmadge, 1976). By 1976 the resulting Title I evaluation and reporting system (TIERS) had taken shape. A *User's Guide* had been developed and distributed (Tallmadge and Wood, 1976). Large-scale training programs for states were begun. A few states began adopting the models immediately. Regional technical assistance centers were established to help states adopt the models. With the help of the regional technical assistance centers more and more states began to use the models until in October 1979, final regulations were in place requiring use of the models and reporting system.

Premises Behind Development of the Models

Wisler and Anderson (1979) have described well the thought that went into development of the models. Their paper is extremely informative, as Anderson was the government's project monitor for the developmental RMC contract and was closely involved with all aspects of the work. The paper lists seven premises behind the development, including:

1. The system should satisfy evaluation needs at the local, state, and federal levels but without necessarily being the sole form of evaluation at any of those levels.
2. The system should focus on summative evaluation of Title I effects on the acquisition of basic skills.
3. The system need not apply uniformly to all Title I subprograms (for example, handicapped, migrant, neglected, or delinquent).
4. The system (for local project evaluations) should not require the use of specific achievement tests.

5. Each applicable Title I project should measure treatment effect as an estimate of how well the program participants performed versus how well they would have performed in the absence of the program.
6. Each applicable Title I project should estimate treatment effects using a USOE evaluation design or an approved alternative that yields comparable results.
7. Each state should report treatment effects to USOE in a common metric.

Most important among these premises is number 5, which defines the nature of the treatment effect. This definition is consistent with the way a statistician defines a treatment effect (see Rubin, 1977), although it is less precise than the statistician might want. This is a practical concession to the field, as school district evaluators often have neither the expertise nor the desire to adopt statistically rigorous designs.

The choice of any evaluation model should be based on "the decisions that will be made as a consequence of the data" (Popham, 1975, p. 196). Each of the models assumes that the primary issue of study is the value of Title I instruction as a supplementary program. Clearly, this was the motivation expressed by Congress and administration policy makers prior to development of the models. But at the same time, the models were not to be restrictive. They were designed to give Congress the information it wanted, but local districts could augment the models however they saw fit. For example, if a district wished to do formative evaluation or use a goal-attainment paradigm, it was encouraged to do so as long as one of the evaluation models was also applied. The federal regulations are quite specific on this matter. "Although the required models are concerned with only the most common Title I objectives — achievement gains in reading, language arts, and mathematics — SEAs and LEAs are encouraged to evaluate all of their project objectives and to collect whatever data are needed for local decision making" (*Federal Register,* October 12, 1979). The models also do not restrict the type of test used, nor do they restrict the evaluation design. As long as a methodology could provide an estimate of treatment effect compatible with premise 5 and in the metric prescribed, it could be found acceptable.

The Models

Work on the models culminated in 1976 with USOE issuing a *User's Guide* (Tallmadge and Wood, 1976), in which the models and reporting metric were described. Three general models were proposed: a norm-referenced model, a control group model, and a regression model. They were given the labels A, B, and C respectively. Most state and local evaluators refer to them by their letter designations.

The norm-referenced model, or Model A, is the model that most resembles current evaluation designs. It is a pretest-posttest design with growth judged in terms of gains in percentile rank from pretest to posttest. For example, if a group of Title I students had both pre- and posttest scores at the twentieth percentile rank one concludes there has been no impact. If the post-test score rose from the twentieth to the twenty-fifth percentile rank one concludes there has been a positive impact. In this model, the national norms act as a surrogate comparison group. Without Title I, students are presumed to remain at the same percentile rank in the national norms on pretest and post-test. To reduce the size of the regression effect one encounters in using gain scores, districts were required to not select students for the program on the basis of the pretest scores. Studies by Roberts (1980) indicated that such an empirical procedure would eliminate all but an inconsequential amount of the regression effect. In later refinements to the model, one was allowed to select students on the pretest, with the provision that students be selected solely on the pretest and a statistical correction be applied to the gain to account for unreliability of the test (see McNemar, 1975, p. 169). In theory such a correction will result in gains similar to those when selection is not on the pretest. Most districts use Model A, which is generally regarded by measurement and statistical people as weak. Most of the technical questions raised concerning the models generally involve some aspect of Model A.

The control group model, or Model B, may be either the idealized randomized design or the more common nonequivalent control group design. It too requires pretesting and posttesting. Either the analysis of covariance or Kenny's (1977) standardized change score analysis may be used to obtain treatment effects. This design is rarely used because its use requires withholding Title I services from students who might nominally be expected to receive some compensatory program.

The special regression model, Model C, is a variation of the analysis of covariance first used by Belsen (1956) to evaluate the effects of a television broadcast. Belsen had coined the phrase "method of stable correlates" to describe his procedure. In a later article, Cochran (1970) demonstrated that Belsen's procedure was related to the analysis of covariance. In both procedures the treatment effect is obtained from the pretest and posttest, X and Y, by calculating

$$\bar{Y}_c - \bar{Y}_t - b(\bar{X}_c - \bar{X}_t)$$

where c and t refer to the comparison and treatment groups respectively. The difference between the two methods lies in the way b is estimated. In Belsen's procedure b is an estimate obtained from only the comparison group. In the analysis of covariance b is obtained by pooling sums of squares over the treatment and comparison groups. The procedure given in the *User's Guide* is the same as that of Belsen.

Cochran demonstrates in his paper that Belsen's procedure is preferred when there are substantially more people in the comparison group or when the variance in the treatment group is extremely large and the regression coefficients are equal in the two groups. When the regression coefficients differ, Belsen's procedure is preferred. Model C additionally requires that the pretest be used for selection with a strict cut-off. The pretest might be a composite of several test and judgmental variables, but the selection must be based solely on the pretest. This requirement was necessary because for the model to be unbiased, selection must have taken place on the covariate (see Kenny, 1977, and Rubin, 1977).

Judging from the statistical literature, Model C represents about the best technology that statistical theory has to offer. The model is largely untried, however, and its primary assumption — that the pretest and posttest have a linear relationship — may overstate the case. Extrapolating regression lines as is done in Model C is dangerous under any circumstance. It is especially so when a linear function is fit to nonlinear data.

Although there are only three models, there are two versions of each model. One version uses normed tests; the other version uses nonnormed tests. When nonnormed tests are used, a normed test must be administered to the treatment group. This is necessary because nonnormed-score gains must be expressed in terms of gains on a national norm. In order to obtain such a gain, one must be able to estimate the variance of the nonnormed test for the nation ($\sigma_{\eta\eta}^2$). It can be estimated from the following relationship

$$\frac{S_{\eta\eta}^2}{\sigma_{\eta\eta}^2} = \frac{S_\eta^2}{\sigma_\eta^2}$$

where the subscripts denote normed and nonnormed tests, σ^2 is the national variance, and S^2 is the variance in the school district. Since S_η^2 and $S_{\eta\eta}^2$ are observed and σ_η^2 is obtained from the test publisher's manual, $\sigma_{\eta\eta}^2$ can be estimated. Gains on the nonnormed test can then be expressed in terms of standard score gains on a nationally normed test scale.

The common metric, the normal curve equivalent or NCE, requires that all score gains must be expressed in terms of gain on a national norm. The NCE scale is a normalized standard-score scale that divides the distance between the first and ninety-ninth percentile under a normal curve into ninety-eight equal units. The metric is similar to the stanine metric, but is finer graded to pick up small shifts in achievement.

The models are comparable in the sense that each results in an NCE gain. NCE gains are aggregated across districts by grade level, resulting in a state report. Separate aggregations are made for nine-month evaluations (fall and spring testing) and for twelve-month evaluations (annual fall or annual spring testing). Results from the state reports are aggregated by the Department of Education for their report to Congress.

Three Models, Two Models, One Model?

In 1978 our technical assistance center took an informal survey of other technical assistance centers and state education departments to find out how many school districts were using Model B for Title I evaluation. Much to our surprise, we could find only six instances in which the model had been used, and in three of those instances, the school districts were no longer willing to continue with the model.

Why was this so? After some discussion the answer became clear. In general, Title I does not exist independently of other compensatory education programs. In many instances districts are required to serve all students who are judged to be "in need," regardless of the student's school. If a student is not eligible under Title I, a state program provides compensatory services. In other instances school districts will go to extraordinary means to see that all of the eligible poor achieving students are placed in Title I. What this means is that in many school districts, there are no students comparable with Title I students who are not receiving some type of compensatory program. There are just no "untreated" students in most school districts, rendering Model B infeasible for most districts.

This is not to say that Model B is infeasible for all districts. In a few school districts, those whose Title I allocation is small in relation to the district's achievement level, some schools in the district have achievement levels similar to Title I schools but because of economic criteria are not eligible for Title I, or if they are eligible they do not have enough money for any compensatory program. These districts might use the model. Nevertheless, such instances are rare, and there may be important confounding variables included in the results of an analysis of this type. For these reasons, only a handful of districts consider the model.

On a practical level we are left with two models, Model A and Model C. But experience with Model C has been disappointing. The model rests on the assumption that without treatment the relationship between pretest and posttest is linear. This assumption is not entirely unreasonable, and any search of the educational evaluation literature will reveal that it is often made. Yet when we examine Model C analyses we often find nonlinear data. Nonlinearities often come to light in studies comparing Model A with Model C. For example, in 1978 Florida compared the NCE gains of districts using Models A and C (Hardy, 1979). Although the Model A results showed a positive effect for Title I, the Model C results were clustered about zero with a wide variation. In RMC's secondary analysis of data from the sustained effects study (see Carter, 1980) when Model C was applied to an untreated data set, consisting of student data from schools without compensatory programs, large positive NCE gains were found. Finding a large negative effect in Model C analysis is not uncommon judging from the Model C analyses our technical assistance center has seen.

Generally, all these findings can be traced to measurement problems. Floor effects, ceiling effects, or both make their way into either the pretest or posttest. Nonlinear data result. Even a moderate degree of nonlinearity can have an enormous effect on the results since the no-treatment expectation that is used to obtain the NCE gain requires extrapolating the regression line developed from a restricted range of pretest and posttest scores in the comparison group. Poor test administration practice or poor motivation on the part of students also accounts for errors in the analysis by creating outliers that either suppress or steepen the comparison group's regression slope.

Model C also requires a great deal of work, as many scores need to be matched and analyzed. Title I evaluators are accustomed to matching scores for Title I students, but they lack experience in matching scores for the comparison group, which is two to ten times larger. Practically speaking, to do a good job of analysis with Model C one must have access to a computer and have some experience in performing and interpreting regression analyses. Few school districts have these capabilities.

That Model C does not seem to work uniformly well for Title I evaluation is not a problem confined to TIERS. It has implications for all educational evaluations attempting to use statistical methods and quasi-experiments. If there are measurement problems that result in floor and ceiling effects for local analysis, how good are the conventional approaches we use in national evaluations that emphasize linear relationships and continuous measurement? The same tests are used by local school districts as are used by those doing large-scale national evaluations. Even in large-scale, carefully planned, national evaluations, tests are administered by the classroom teacher. Other mathematical functions can be fit in the regressions, but how often does one see this in national evaluations?

The notion of information from item-response theory may be useful in telling us something about the form of the regressions we seek. Information is akin to the inverse of the standard error of estimate for a given ability level. Information is not constant, but varies with ability level. We might expect a regression function to be linear in a neighborhood of ability when its information is above a certain level. Knowledge of the information function for a test may tell us which part of the data we should censor in a linear analysis. Further research into the relationship between the characteristics of the tests used to measure achievement and the statistical method used to manipulate the scores would prove helpful.

Experience with the models has shown a gradual decrease in the number of districts using Model C. With the recent Model A refinement that selection can be based on the pretest score, it would seem that the death knell for Model C has rung, and we find ourselves not with three models, but now with only one.

Philosophical and Technical Issues

Since 1976, when technical assistance centers began and state departments of education were trained in the use of the models and the reporting system, issues have been raised about Title I evaluation and the RMC models. Both technical and philosophical issues have come to the forefront. On the philosophical front, controversy has raged over the general approach used. Should a national longitudinal study be commissioned, or should existing local evaluation data be used? The U.S. Office of Education (USOE) had commissioned the sustaining effects study, a large-scale national study of the effects of compensatory education, performed by the Systems Development Corporation. This study is a systematic, carefully controlled study begun in 1974 as a successor to the earlier ETS study. They also routinely collected local district evaluations through state reports. They are going both ways. Congress, however, was clear in its charge to USOE. Cross (1979) reports that the author of the evaluation section of the 1974 amendments wanted to "strengthen state and local evaluation capabilities and gather comparable data." The law was specific on the matter of national evaluations. Section 183(i) of P. L. 93-380 states, "In carrying out the provisions of this section, the Commissioner shall place priority on assisting states, local education agencies, and state agencies to conduct evaluations, and shall, only as funds are available after fulfilling that purpose, seek to conduct any national evaluations of the program."

Cross (1979) has noted that "a number of academicians have charged that Congress is not affected by data or program information." Title I is the largest federal program in elementary and secondary education. More than 90 percent of the nation's school districts receive Title I funds. These funds, for the most part, pay teacher and administrator salaries. A reporting system based on estimating impact represents a threat to those people. If no evidence of program impact were found, as had happened in past studies, there could be a drive to reduce Title I funding, especially when efforts are being made to reduce government spending.

Supporters of Title I believe that any good evaluation system would support their notion that Title I was working. Many people who had been involved with Title I evaluation were less optimistic that demonstrating impact would have much effect on Title I funding. For these people, a good evaluation system was one that helped to improve programs rather than justify them. Formative and process evaluations were to be preferred over summative and outcome evaluations. Because the RMC models stressed summative outcome evaluation and made no mention of formative or process evaluation, the RMC models were viewed skeptically by those who held this view.

The Congressional mandate was clearly to strengthen state and local evaluation practice by requiring use of the best technology that the Office of Education could develop. Some of the larger states, however, believed that their current level of evaluation technology was of sufficient quality or better quality than that of USOE. To these states, the issue was the extent USOE could force evaluation policy onto the states. They resisted the system until regulations for evaluation were written, making the law in effect for Title I evaluation.

On the technical front, the issues were more numerous and specific to the methodologies RMC had proposed. These issues were raised by technical assistance center staff, academics, and the more technically sophisticated among state and local evaluators. Issues were specific to the way in which the models are used. For example, there were a whole host of issues surrounding Model A. An outline of the various issues follows:

Model A Issues.
- How valid is the assumption that students will maintain their percentile status in the norms group without Title I?
- How important is it to use the same test level and form for pretest and posttest?
- To what extent does requiring that different test administrations be used for pretesting and posttesting eliminate the regression effect?
- Can statistical adjustments rather than separate testings for selection and pretesting be used to reduce the regression effect?

Model C Issues
- What is the effect of using different selection procedures in different buildings on the impact estimate?
- How stable is the estimate?

Nonnormed test models
- How accurate is the conversion of gains to the NCE metric?
- How adequate is Model A2?

General measurement issues
- What effects are introduced as a result of test interlevel articulation?
- How can the evaluation models be used to measure summer growth?
- What is the effect of student attrition on impact estimates?
- How strong is the practice effect in Title I data?
- How can we identify outliers in data?
- What NCE gains are educationally significant?
- How valid are scores below the first percentile?

The above issues have spawned many an AERA paper over the last three years. An informal count of the numbers of papers given at AERA in 1978 and 1979 on the evaluation models showed twenty-eight and forty-nine papers respectively. The technical issues listed above are also the subject of a contract awarded to RMC in 1978 to refine the system they proposed in 1976. Separate papers dealing with each issue are planned and should be available in 1981.

The most serious issue has both philosophical and technical aspects. It involves the comparability of results over different evaluation designs. Section 183(f) of the law (P.L. 93-380) required that the models will specify "techniques . . . for producing data which are comparable on a statewide and nationwide basis." Of course, this was to be the remedy for past evaluation failures, where the data reported from states could not be pulled together because they were not comparable. But what does it mean to have comparable results? On the one hand, many studies have demonstrated that the models do not produce comparable results, at least when comparable is defined as being exactly the same NCE gain as when using a different methodology (see Echternacht, 1978; Jaeger, 1978, for two examples). Even those who developed the system recognize that. Their studies, however, seem to indicate that the models do produce similar results, that is, results that generally lead to the same conclusion, even though the actual NCE gains may differ. For example, Roberts (1980) reports results that Model A gains may contain some regression to the mean, but that bias accounts for less than .05 of a standard deviation, an amount unlikely to affect any general conclusion about the overall effect of Title I.

Reporting to Congress

Although the Title I evaluation system is designed to provide useful data at both the local and federal levels, its primary function is to provide comparable data for a report to Congress on the effectiveness of the program. The first use of this data is made in a recent report from the Office of Program

Evaluation. Evidence of Title I program effectiveness is taken from two sources. The primary data source is the sustaining effects study (Carter, 1980). The general findings from this study indicate a small positive effect for Title I.

Data collected through TIERS is used as a secondary source to substantiate findings from the sustaining effects study. NCE gains reported by twenty-three states who voluntarily used the evaluation models during the 1977–1978 school year are interpreted. Data from an early draft of that report appear in Table 1. These unedited, preliminary data were given only to illustrate how the results from TIERS are likely to be presented to Congress. A final version of this report is as yet unavailable.

Before looking more closely at these data, some cautions are in order. States and local districts were just beginning to use the evaluation models in 1977. The quality of data reported, which had been at issue in prior national evaluations of Title I, may also be poor in this instance. For example, in only five states was it known that policies had been adopted not allowing local districts to select students based on the pretest results.

The data in the table are reported in NCE units for reading. The difference between the columns labeled *Normal Growth* and *Title I Growth* is the NCE gain for the twenty-three reporting states. Note that an NCE gain is not actually presented. Instead, NCE gains are interpreted in terms of a percentage of normal growth. Thus, for second grade, one concludes Title I students grew 57 percent more than they would have had they not been in Title I.

This type of interpretation is necessary when reporting NCE gains to the untrained. In theory an NCE gain of zero means that students did not grow any more than one would normally expect. This is often interpreted by the untrained as meaning that these students "learned nothing." One must show that students do grow in achievement through the year and compare actual growth with that standard. A local district makes the same type of interpretation when it uses the test publisher's standard scores. Standard scores cannot be used directly at the national level since different tests use different standard score scales.

More should be said about the way in which "normal growth" was obtained in the table. The methodology was developed by Tallmadge and Fagan (1977) in a working paper. A variation of this methodology has also

Table 1. Title I Gains in Reading Based on 23 State Reports for 1977–1978

Grade	N	Normal Growth	Title I Growth	% Additional Growth
2	93,723	20.4	32.0	57
3	83,697	13.9	21.4	54
4	73,923	13.7	21.1	54
5	67,314	11.0	16.5	50
6	55,982	9.6	12.0	25
7	32,660	6.7	11.4	70
8	23,104	7.9	12.4	57

been proposed by Stenner and others (1978). Since reporting formats were not standardized at the time the state data were reported, only NCE gains were reported by all states. Evidence from the earlier ETS study of compensatory education indicated that the typical Title I student scored at the twentieth percentile rank. Corresponding scaled scores were obtained for this percentile assuming a spring pretest. Corresponding scaled scores were then obtained for the same percentile assuming a spring posttest one year later. The difference between the two scaled scores was designated as normal growth and recorded in terms of scaled scores. This was standardized by dividing each gain by the third-grade standard deviation. The result was multiplied by the standard deviation of the NCE distribution to give "normal growth" in terms of NCE units. This was repeated with four different scale score metrics from different standardized achievement tests. The results were averaged by grade to give the normal growth figure in the table for each grade. Title I growth is obtained by adding the NCE gain to the normal growth.

This method of reporting scores raises a number of technical issues brought about because there is no national scale applied to school achievement. The method relies on assumptions about the nature of growth, the nature of the testing that took place, and the accuracy of the results reported. Although these assumptions may be reasonable, they are largely unsubstantiated by research findings.

Nevertheless, the reported results convey a clear message intended for the nonscientific reader. Although one can point to the technical flaws made in the construction of the table, the essential features conform to prior beliefs. For example, the numbers presented for normal growth in reading generally conform to how we believe growth to be. It is largest in the lower grades, tapering off as students become older. Although NCE gains are largest in the lower grades, the percent of growth attributable to Title I is roughly the same for all grades. This type of interpretation is important because people often conclude erroneously that because NCE gains in the lower grades are typically higher than those for the higher grades, Title I must be more effective in the lower grades. That may be a true statement, but TIERS data neither substantiate nor belie that claim.

Data from TIERS do suggest that the effect of Title I is greater than the effect reported in the sustaining effects study. NCE gains from those five states with specific policies against local districts using the pretest for selecting students are considerably smaller than those for the group as a whole. Nevertheless, this suggests that the data reported in the table overestimate the actual gain by some unknown amount.

TIERS in Evolution

The Title I evaluation system has not been static. It has evolved based on the experience of states and local school districts using the evaluation models and on the research of many who have been associated with Title I evaluation. The changes can be noted by comparing the 1976 version of the *User's Guide* (Tallmadge and Wood, 1976) with the draft policy manual (Office of

Planning and Evaluation, 1980) which also describes the model rules and testing recommendations. For example, in the 1976 *User's Guide,* the requirements for Model A include not using the pretest for selection, using the same form and level of test for pretest and posttest, and an emphasis on testing students at their functional level. In the draft policy manual we find a statistical correction for when the pretest is used for selection, an emphasis on duplicating testing practices used by publishers when they normed their tests, and slightly less emphasis on functional level testing.

More changes will occur, although they will be changes in practice at the local and state levels rather than changes in the actual model rules. More states will use sampling. States must now develop sampling plans for three-year evaluation cycles. In these sampling plans states set schedules for having their local districts report evaluation results. Local districts may be required to report evaluation results each year, or they may be required to report only once in three years. This decision rests with the individual state. Local districts may also use sampling at each grade level in their evaluations. Sampling plans developed by local districts must be acceptable to the state.

Local school districts and the federal government generally support sampling. States generally resist sampling. Federal support is implied by the issuing of a handbook on sampling (Shoemaker, 1978) providing specific methodologies that local districts can use. Local support comes from the feeling that testing must be reduced and that reporting is more a burden to them than a help. States oppose sampling because they use the annual evaluation results to monitor the Title I program. For example, the number of students a district claims to have served is often compared with the number of students tested as a check on enrollments.

Nonetheless, sampling will be used more frequently because it results in less manipulation of data. With sampling states find that their reports to the federal government are easier to prepare. Because there are fewer data, quality can be monitored more easily. Reports become more timely.

More strains are being placed on district testing programs. Tests are being asked to do more. In some instances the same test must serve as the test for evaluation, placement in the program, for diagnosis, and for state minimum basic skills. Consolidation of these testing programs will continue. States are equating their tests for basic skills testing with a nationally standardized test so that national percentiles can be reported for each examinee. Tests are being advertised by publishers as both norm-referenced and criterion-referenced, usable for both diagnosis and program evaluation. At the same time, test publishers are developing shorter tests. For example, in the widely used California Achievement Test usually given at fourth grade, the number of vocabulary items has been reduced from forty items in level three of the 1970 edition to thirty items in level fourteen of the 1977 edition. Reading comprehension items have been reduced from forty-two to forty.

The effect of consolidating so much testing and shortening the tests is to reduce the effectiveness of the test for many of the purposes it must serve. Tests used as minimum competency tests for a state may not work well for evaluation. Tests selected for their ability to diagnose student needs will not necessarily be good tests for program evaluation.

A final trend associated with TIERS has been an increasing emphasis on using the information resulting from applying the evaluation models. In choosing between a national evaluation of Title I and using the locally developed evalutions, an argument often given is that national evaluations are not useful locally, while locally performed evaluations are. Since TIERS is a local evaluation system, much effort has gone into developing ways to make the information useful at the local level. This effort has had two results. First, the statistical issues associated with the models have been placed on a back burner. In general, those issues are not unique to TIERS, but pervade all evaluation practice. The feeling among those who work in Title I evaluation is that these issues will be with us no matter what the evaluation approach. Second, fundamental notions of evaluation are being stressed—for example, identifying evaluation audiences, explaining results, and identifying who needs what types of information and why. The evaluation models are viewed as one small piece of information at the local level. Formative evaluation and complete use of test results are being viewed as equal in importance to the outcome results eventually reported to Congress.

References

Belsen, W. A. "A Technique for Studying the Effects of a Television Broadcast." *Applied Statistics,* 1956, *5,* 195–202.

Bessey, B., Rosen, L., Chiang, A., and Tallmadge, G. "Further Documentation of State ESEA Title I Reporting Models and Their Technical Assistance Requirements." Mountain View, Calif.: RMC Research Corporation, 1976.

Carter, L. "The Sustaining Effects Study: An Interim Report." Santa Monica, Calif.: Systems Development Corp., 1980.

Cochran, W. "The Use of Covariance in Observational Studies." *Applied Statistics,* 1970, *18,* 270–275.

Cross, C. "Title I Evaluation—A Case Study in Congressional Frustration." *Educational and Policy Analysis,* 1979, *1,* (2), 15–21.

Echternacht, G. "The Use of Different Models in the ESEA Title I Evaluation System." Paper presented at annual AERA meeting, Toronto, 1978.

Federal Register, Oct. 12, 1979.

Gamel, N., Tallmadge, G., Wood, C., and Binkley, J. "State ESEA Title I Reports: Review and Analysis of Past Reports and Development of a Model Reporting System and Format." Mountain View, Calif.: RMC Research Corporation, 1975.

Hardy, R. A. "Comparison of Model A and Model C: Results of First-Year Implementation in Florida." Educational Testing Service, unpublished paper, January 1979.

Hendrickson, G. "Review of Title I Evaluation Studies. DHEW Office of the Assistant Secretary for Planning and Evaluation," 1978.

Jaeger, R. M. "On Combining Achievement Test Data Through NCE Scaled Scores." Paper presented at annual Conference of Directors of State Testing Programs, Princeton, N.J., 1978.

Kenny, D. "A Quasi-Experimental Approach to Assessing Treatment Effects in Nonequivalent Control Group Designs." *Psychological Bulletin,* 1977, *82* (3), 345–362.

McLaughlin, M. *Evaluation and Reform: The Elementary and Secondary Education Act of 1965.* New York: Ballinger, 1975.

McNemar, Q. *Psychological Evaluation.* Englewood Cliffs, N.J.: Prentice-Hall, 1975.

Office of Planning and Evaluation. "Evaluation." In *Draft Policy Manual.* Washington, D.C.: Department of Education, September 5, 1980.

Popham, W. *Educational Evaluation.* Englewood Cliffs, N.J.: Prentice-Hall, 1975.

Roberts, O. A. *Regression to the Mean and Regression-Effect Bias.* Mountain View, Calif.: RMC Research Corporation, 1980.

Rubin, D. "Assignment to Treatment Group or the Basis of a Covariate." *Journal of Educational Statistics,* 1977, *2* (1), 1–26.

Shoemaker, D. "Use of Sampling Procedures with the USOE Title I Evaluation Models." Washington, D.C.: Office of Evaluation and Dissemination, USOE, 1978.

Stenner, A., Hunter, E., Bland, J., and Cooper, L. "The Standardized Growth Expectation: Implications for Educational Evaluation." Paper presented at annual AERA meeting, Toronto, 1978.

Tallmadge, G., and Fagan, B. "Cognitive Growth and Growth Expectations in Reading and Mathematics: A Working Paper." Mountain View, Calif.: RMC Research Corporation, 1977.

Tallmadge, G., and Wood, C. *User's Guide: ESEA Title I Evaluation and Reporting System.* Mountain View, Calif.: RMC Research Corporation, 1976.

Thomas, T., and Pelavin, S. "Patterns in ESEA Title I Reading Achievement." Menlo Park, Calif.: Stanford Research Institute, 1976.

U.S. Office of Education. "Financial Assistance to Local Educational Agencies to Meet the Special Educational Needs of Educationally Deprived and Neglected and Delinquent Children—Evaluation Requirements." *Federal Register,* October 12, 1979, *44* (199), 59152–59159.

Wargo, M. Tallmadge, G., Michaels, P., Fipe, D., and Morris, S. "ESEA Title I: A Reanalysis and Synthesis of Evaluation Data from Fiscal Year 1965 through 1970." Palo Alto, Calif.: American Institutes for Research, 1972.

Washington Research Project, and NAACP Legal Defense and Educational Fund. "Title I of ESEA: Is It Helping Poor Children?" Washington, D.C.: Washington Research Project, December 1969.

Wisler, C., and Anderson, J. "Designing a Title I Evaluation System to Meet Legislative Requirements." *Educational Evaluation and Policy Analysis,* 1979, *1,* 47–55.

Gary Echternacht is director of the Region II, ESEA Title I Technical Assistance Center for the Educational Testing Service, Princeton, N.J.

*Internal validity is rarely considered by users of the Title I Evaluation
and Reporting System because of the system's mandatory nature.
Such disregard can result in inaccurate interpretations
of impact data.*

Internal Validity of the ESEA Title I Evaluation Models

Steve Murray
Judy Arter

The Title I Evaluation and Reporting System (TIERS) is a means of standardizing Title I evaluation practice and reporting at the local and state level. Nationwide use of the TIERS for Title I projects in reading, language arts, and mathematics from grade two through grade twelve is intended to facilitate understanding of the effects of Title I projects at local, state, and national levels. It is expected that the resulting evaluation information will be technically sound and comparable across projects.

At the heart of the TIERS are three evaluation models, any one of which can be used to estimate the impact of a local Title I project on the achievement of the students served (Tallmadge and Wood, 1976). Each of the three models can be used with normed or nonnormed tests, giving six options from which a local Title I project evaluator may choose.

Implementing any one of the models results in a measure of project impact, the treatment effect, which is intended to measure how much the Title I project contributed to student achievement. Each model involves a different method of generating a no-treatment expectation — an estimate of how project students would have performed without the project but with regular school instruction. The no-treatment expectation is compared to observed performance upon completion of the project. The difference between the no-treatment expectation and actual performance defines the treatment effect.

Comparable reporting on achievement is facilitated through a common reporting metric, the Normal Curve Equivalent (NCE). The NCE is a normalized standard score with a mean of 50 and a standard deviation of 21.06. It is generally understood that the NCE is based upon nationally representative grade level norms.

Adoption of the TIERS evaluation models as standard practice in Title I evaluation has prompted technical commentary and research projects on a number of methodological issues. A number of state departments of education have conducted small-scale research projects refining various aspects of the TIERS. Using available large-scale data bases, the RMC Research Corporation has investigated a number of technical issues that bear on sound use of the TIERS. Other researchers have accounted for hundreds of papers examining technical issues. Concerns have covered such topics as test development and standardization procedures, test floor and ceiling effects, regression to the mean, and bias in the measures of treatment effect resulting from the implementation of each of the evaluation models.

Criticisms of the TIERS in general and each of the evaluation models in particular can be analyzed with reference to the threat that they pose to making valid inferences from results of applying the models. Cook and Campbell (1976) have identified five classes of validity against which various experimental or quasi-experimental designs may be evaluated. These threats to validity include:

1. *Internal validity:* the extent to which inferences of cause-effect relationships systematically and appropriately reject rival alternative causes.

2. *Statistical conclusion validity:* the extent to which statistically based conclusions about the existence of covariation are free from Type I and Type II errors.

3. *External validity:* the extent to which results may be expected to generalize soundly across persons, settings, and times.

4. *Construct validity of cause:* the extent to which operational definitions, either through manipulations or measurements, of independent variables are unambiguously interpretable at a given level of reduction.

5. *Construct validity of effects:* the extent to which operational definitions of dependent variables are unambiguously interpretable at a given level of reduction.

Although technical investigations on TIERS have implications for all five types of validity, this paper will concentrate on the threats to internal validity posed by the three TIERS evaluation models. (For a more complete discussion of all five threats to validity, see Murray, Arter, and Faddis, 1979). The internal validity threats to be considered here have been enumerated by Cook and Campbell (1976) as follows: (1) *history:* events that are not a part of the "treatment" and which take place between a pretest and a posttest may affect the dependent variable; (2) *maturation:* spontaneous or natural development of a respondent during the treatment; (3) *testing:* effects due to test taking a number of times; (4) *instrumentation:* effects due to changes in the measuring instrument; (5) *statistical regression:* effects due to the selection of extreme groups as an experimental or control group; (6) *selection:* effects due to differences in the kinds of persons in the experimental or control group; (7) *mortality:* effects due to subjects dropping out of the experiment before its completion; (8) *interactions with selection:* effects due to the interaction of history, maturity, mortality, and so on, with selection; (9) *ambiguity about the direction of influence:* effects of A and B are clouded by research that does not clearly allow for testing of the direction of causality; (10) *diffusion or imitation of the treatment:* effects of the control group's adoption of procedures that are also part of the treatment; (11) *compensatory equalization of the treatment:* effects of adding resources to control groups as an administrative or political device for providing equity; (12) *compensatory rivalry:* competition effects resulting from public declaration of membership in either experimental or control groups; (13) *resentful demoralization of respondents receiving less desirable treatments:* differences due to response of resentment on the part of respondents; (14) *local history:* effects of group-specific events in treatment or testing.

Model A: Threats to Internal Validity

Model A, the norm-referenced model, uses the norms of a test to generate the no-treatment expectation. It is assumed that without supplemental help, students would maintain their percentile status over time (the equipercentile growth assumption). The no-treatment expectation is the percentile equivalent of the average pretest score for the group. This is compared to posttest percentile status to produce the measure of treatment effect. Model A is by far the most frequently implemented of the available alternatives.

Because of its originality as a quasi-experimental design, Model A is easily the least studied of the three evaluation models making up the TIERS. The methodological development of the comparison group model (Model B) has been traced to the early part of this century (Campbell and Stanley, 1966). Refinements to the comparison group design are still being advanced (see Cronbach, Rogosa, Ploden, and Price, 1976). Model C, an extrapolation of the regression-discontinuity design introduced by Thistlewaite and Campbell (1960), has a history of nearly twenty years. By comparison, Model A is a very recent addition to the list of quasi-experimental designs. Consequently, little work on Model A has yet been published.

Model A is fundamentally nonanalytic. That is, there is no explicit statistical model to support its application for projecting unbiased no-treatment expectations. On the other hand, both Model B and Model C are based on formal statistical models with well-known assumptions. Attempts to develop a statistical rationale for a norm-referenced model have resulted in approaches to generating unbiased no-treatment expectations that conflict with the originally proposed Model A (Burton, 1979; Echternacht, 1978; Murray, 1978, 1979). The absence of a formal statistical model suggests a basic ambiguity of Model A and inhibits definitive critique.

An analysis of Model A in terms of threats to internal validity must take into account the use of norms as the basis for the evaluation metric and as a substitute for a comparison group. Many of the technical issues concerning Model A may be classified as threats resulting from variations in instrumentation. These issues include the effects of sampling errors in norms, equating errors, interpolation and extrapolation errors, and score transformation errors. Errors of these types can lead to biased results in specific project evaluations.

Additional threats to validity can be related to the use of norms as a pseudo comparison group. The pseudo comparison group is a subgroup of the norm group that scores at exactly the same level as the local Title I group on the pretest. The pseudo comparison group is assumed to maintain its percentile status from pretest time to posttest time. The pseudo comparison group cannot, in actuality, be identified within the norm groups.

These introductory remarks should help in understanding the various internal validity threats characteristic of Model A.

History. According to Campbell and Stanley (1966, p. 5), history as a threat to internal validity, is "the specific events occurring between the first and second measurement in addition to the experimental variable." In Model A the effect of historical happenings is unknown, since, for the comparison group, the norms were developed at a different time and in a variety of locations rather than the specific location of the single group of Title I students. Since the norm group may not have been equally affected by extraneous events, the norms do not provide a control for them.

Maturation. Students change over time simply as a result of getting older. Norms take this maturation into account at a gross level. In essence, norms account for the maturation of total populations or random samples of students from such populations. A random sample of students would be expected to score very near the fiftieth percentile on appropriate grade level norms. These same students would also be expected to score at the fiftieth percentile in some subsequent testing also given appropriate grade-level norms. Norms do not necessarily account for maturation of nonrandomly selected students. The equipercentile growth assumption, which is the Model A approach to modeling maturation, applies the general rule for total population maturation on normed tests to any selected subgroup of that population. That is, any selected group is expected to maintain its percentile status from pretest to posttest as long as it was not selected on the pretest. Maturation as a threat to validity is, therefore, closely related to selection and statistical regression. As will be noted in the following discussions of selection and statistical regression, a number of studies have questioned the general application of Model A procedures for control over maturation or statistical regression.

Testing. There may be effects due to test taking a number of times (Roberts, 1980). Students may become testwise or get to know the test, especially if the test is used year after year or used for selection, pretesting, and posttesting. Test scores may increase not because of the project but because the students know the test. Testing effects may be more of a problem in Model A than in the other models because in Models B and C the same effects would tend to appear in the comparison group and the treatment group.

Instrumentation. Instrumentation errors that could affect Model A evaluation results include differential sampling errors in norms, errors resulting from scalar transformations, errors stemming from interpolation and extrap-

olation, errors of equating across levels and between forms, and errors resulting from failure to adhere to standard test administration procedures including failure to test on norm dates. Any of these might result in an over- or
underestimation of the treatment effect (Armor and others, 1976; DeVito and
Long, 1977; Wood, 1978; Scherich, 1978; Slinde and Linn, 1977).

Sampling Error. Error in the national norms occurs when the sample
of students chosen for the norming group is not representative of the national
population. This can happen either as a result of faulty sampling design or
random sampling differences. In either case, sampling error can create errors
in Model A results (Jaeger, undated; Tallmadge and Horst, 1978). Sampling
error could be a biasing factor in the same testing series if the direction and
magnitude of the error is not the same for all grades. For example, if the grade
three sample was slightly more able than the national population and the grade
four sample was slightly less able, then a group of students could have a higher
percentile standing on the third grade than the fourth, even though they
remained the same with respect to the national population. Bias due to sampling error may also be a factor when comparing results across tests for which
sampling errors are different. Several studies (Jaeger, undated; Wood, 1978)
have demonstrated that such sampling errors, while small, are present and can
bias individual project results.

Equipercentile Function. If the equipercentile function (that is, the
pretest standard score against the posttest standard score predicted by the
equipercentile assumption) is not linear, then the unit of analysis (calculating
averages on standard scores and then converting to NCEs versus converting
scores to NCEs first and then averaging) may affect results (Wood, 1978).
One study (Kaskowitz and Norwood, 1977) found the function to be fairly linear for the Metropolitan Achievement Test (MAT). If the equipercentile
assumption is not appropriate for disadvantaged populations, then the
replacement function also needs to be linear.

Interpolation and Extrapolation. When interpolation or extrapolation to test dates are necessary, different methods and assumptions may lead
to different results (Baker and Williams, 1978; Bridgemann, 1978; Conklin,
Burstein, and Keesling, 1979). For example, if testing occurs four weeks
before the fall norm date, norms could be projected either by interpolating
between the previous spring and current fall norms or by extrapolating from
the current fall and next spring norms. These methods yield different results.

Smoothing and Fitting of Empirical Data. This occurs when scores
are equated across forms and levels of a test (as when developing expanded
scale scores). A number of studies have shown that resulting errors tend to be
small but add up in the extremes of the distribution and when testing out of
level and across forms (Crowder, 1978; Friendly, 1980; Fuentes and Jeffress,
1978; Haenn and Proctor, 1978; Hiscox and Owens, 1978; Long, Schaffran,
and Kellogg, 1977; Ozenne, 1978; Powers, 1978; Slaughter and Gallas, 1978;
Slinde and Linn, 1977; Wood, 1978).

Fall-fall (or spring-spring) evaluations routinely give different measures of impact than fall-spring evaluation (David and Pelavin, 1978; DeVito
and Long, 1977; Faddis and Estes, 1978; Hardy, 1979; Holthouse, Stofflet,

and Tokar, 1976; Hammond and Frechtling, 1979; Stenner and Bland, 1979; Wood, 1980b). These differences could be interpreted as a result of differences between the normal maturational process of Title I and regular students (regular students continue to gain when not in school while Title I students do not). Or it may be interpreted as a scaling artifact resulting from assumptions about summer growth in the norms (that is, some students appear to lose ground because an expectation for summer growth is built into the norms). Therefore, assumptions concerning summer growth could affect evaluation results.

Finally, if students are tested with a test that is too easy or too hard, their true status and gain may be under- or overestimated (Faddis and Estes, 1978). The observed evaluation results may therefore not reflect actual gains.

Statistical Regression. Evaluation designs applied to extreme groups such as Title I students are often prone to bias from statistical regression, sometimes called "regression to the mean." When retested, groups selected for their extremity tend to score closer to the mean of the population from which they were selected. Estimates of the regression effect show that when selection of Title I students is based on the pretest, regression is considerable (Mandeville, 1978; Yap, 1978; Stammon, Raffeld, and Powell, 1979).

The "control" for regression effects in Model A is to use one measure to select students and a second measure as a pretest from which the no-treatment expectation is derived. It is assumed that there is not further statistical regression from the pretest to the posttest. However, there have been several demonstrations that this procedure eliminates regression effects only under very unusual circumstances (Burton, 1979; Glass, 1978; Hiscox and Owens, 1978; Murray, 1978).

Although Model A does not necessarily eliminate bias due to statistical regression it will probably reduce such a threat (Glass, 1978; Murray, 1978; Wood, 1980a). Recently, several formulas have been proposed to correct the no-treatment expectation for regression (Echternacht, 1978; Murray, 1978; Powell, Schmidt, and Raffeld, 1979; Wood, 1980b; Yap, 1978). These formulas can be useful when selection is based on a strict cut off on the pretest.

Selection. Errors in estimating impact can occur if the students in the treatment and comparison groups are not similar prior to treatment. In this case the comparison group does not provide a sound no-treatment expectation against which to compare the progress of the treatment students. When a real comparison group is available and the procedure for identifying the treatment and comparison groups is clear, it is possible to appraise the extent of selection effects. Since Model A uses a pseudo comparison group (that is, the subpopulation in the national norms scoring the same on the pretest), it is difficult to determine if Model A controls for selection. Because the pseudo comparison group concept is used to further a maturational hypothesis (that groups maintain their percentile status over time), selection effects can be combined with maturation in a selection × maturation interaction. Other interactions with selection are also possible.

Mortality. Mortality could be a factor in Model A insofar as there is differential mortality: different types of students dropping out of the Title I group and norm groups. Since this is an interaction with selection it will be considered in the next section.

Interactions with Selection. Low-achieving students may be more likely to drop out of school, producing an interaction between *mortality* and *selection*. Consequently, the norm group gets progressively "brighter." If there is a differential mortality between the regular and special programs, that is, if a special program is keeping students in school, the treatment group would tend to fall off in percentile status over time. A study examining this issue failed to find support for the hypothesis (Arter and Estes, 1978).

Kaskowitz (1980) also looked at the effect of attrition in low-achieving populations and found that attrition will only make a differences in those cases where attrition is high and the differences in gain between those who leave and those who stay is large.

Instrumentation and Selection. Two interactions can occur. The first is that learning and maturation curves for local treatment students may differ from those of the norm group, implying a selection × maturation effect. Instead of maintaining percentile status, Title I students may indeed fall progressively further behind with time (Linn, 1978). A number of longitudinal studies bearing on the tenability of the equipercentile assumption on various average and low scoring populations show mixed results (Armor and others, 1976; Coleman and others, 1966; Crane and Cech, 1979; Doherty, 1976; Faddis and Arter, 1979; Faddis and Estes, 1978; Hiscox and Owens, 1978; Holthouse, Stofflet, and Tokar, 1976; House, 1979; Kaskowitz and Norwood, 1977; Mayeske and Beaton, 1975; Powell, Schmidt, and Raffeld, 1979; Stenner and Bland, 1979; Stenner, Hunter, Bland, and Cooper, 1978; Storlie, Rice, Harvey, and Crane, 1979; Storlie, Rice, Johnson, and Crowe, 1979; Hammond and Frechtling, 1979; Powers, 1979; Norwood and Stearnes, 1976; O. A. Roberts, 1980a; Wood, 1980a). In general, findings suggest that many things can affect the maintenance of percentile status, and that ideally one should check its accuracy locally.

The second instrumentation by selection involves the use of cross-sectional norms by publishers (norming in all grades at the same time) rather than longitudinal norms (testing the same students as they progress through grades). The result is that even though each grade sample represents the national population at that grade, the students in each grade are different. Thus, the pre- and postcomparison groups for a program may be more or less similar to the constant Title I group (Hiscox and Owens, 1978; Kaskowitz and Norwood, 1977). Estimates of percentile status may change merely because the norm group is changing. Kaskowitz and Norwood (1977) found a reasonably good fit between cross-sectional and longitudinal norms for the MAT.

Testing at times other than norm dates and not following instructions exactly can also result in testing by selection interactions. Since the norm group acts as a pseudo comparison group in Model A, testing off norm dates makes incorrect comparisons of status. Not following test instructions results in noncomparable testing conditions, rendering comparisons of status ambiguous.

Diffusion or Imitation of the Treatment. Excluding Title I students from norming procedures is not a standard practice. To the extent that treatment effects are included in the norms, impact estimates can be artificially low.

Model B: Threats to Validity

Model B is the classic comparison group model. A comparison group is chosen that is as much like the Title I group as possible. The posttest performance of the comparison group (which may be adjusted for differences in pretest status) is used as the no-treatment expectation. The difference between the Title I and comparison groups' adjusted posttest scores is the measure of program treatment effect. When so implemented, Model B is relatively free from threats to internal validity. Its properties have been discussed at length by Campbell and Stanley (1966) and Cook and Campbell (1976). The comparison group model in the TIERS assumes that a reasonable comparison group has been found and that the appropriate method of analysis has been selected. The following discussion will focus on some common threats to validity when Model B cannot be properly implemented. Most of these problems occur because of the difficulty of setting up good control groups in a natural setting.

History and Testing. These factors should present little threat even if selection is not optimum, because both treatment and control groups are local. History and testing effects could only be a source of error if they interact with selection because of some atypical arrangement.

Maturation, Statistical Regression, and Mortality. These should not be sources of error if selection proceeds in the same manner for both the treatment and comparison groups and if the resulting groups appear to be similar on educationally relevant factors. If selection is not reasonable, then these items may affect results to the extent that they are different between groups.

Instrumentation. When a nonnormed test is used in Models B or C, computations are necessary (using the RMC framework) to convert results to NCEs. The first step is to estimate the standard deviation of the national population on the nonnormed test using the formula:

$$\frac{SD_{N,NN}}{SD_{L,NN}} = \frac{SD_{N,NRT}}{SD_{L,NRT}}$$

$$\text{or } SD_{N,NN} = \frac{SD_{N,NRT} \times SD_{L,NN}}{SD_{L,NRT}}$$

NN = nonnormed test
NRT = normed test
N = national population
L = local population

Then $SD_{N,NN}$ is used to make a linear conversion to NCEs:

$$\text{NCE gain} = \frac{21.06}{SD_{N,NN}} (T_2 - C_2)$$

T_2 = X for Title I group on posttest
C_2 = X for Comparison group on posttest

There is some evidence that $SD_{N,NN}$ as computed can be very misleading (Fishbein, 1978; Long, Horwitz, and DeVito, 1978; Pellegrini, Horwitz, and Long, 1979). A study by Klibanoff (1980), however, found that the procedure is unbiased.

Selection. Ideally, selection should proceed through random assignment. In many instances random assignment in Title I projects would be illegal since the lowest-scoring students must be served in Title I. Close approximations to the random assignment can occur when: (1) Students are in the program for one semester and only half the students are served at any one time (students may be randomly assigned to Title I or comparison groups each semester, and the evaluation could be for the first semester only); (2) if only enough money exists for some eligible schools to be served, then the others could serve as comparison schools (the evaluator should give particular attention to differential regression and the comparability of regular school programs); (3) if some students are eligible for Title I classes but do not enroll (as at the high school level) they may be a comparison group, *if* it appears that the reasons they did not enroll make them noncomparable to treatment students. For example, voluntary enrollment might yield different types of students while scheduling problems might not. If groups are random or random-in-effect (Tallmadge and Wood, 1976), Model B calls for covariance or no adjustment depending on the difference between groups on the pretest.

Model B also provides an analysis when treatment and comparison groups are assumed to hail from different populations, resulting in a nonequivalent control group design. Posttest scores are adjusted using a standardized gain score technique or the principal axis adjustment. The principal axis adjustment assumes that without treatment, students will maintain their relative positions through time. If this hypothesis is false, then the principal axis adjustment will be biased (Hiscox and Owens, 1978; Holthouse, Stofflet, and Tokar, 1976; Kaskowitz and Norwood, 1977; Linn, 1978; Norwood and Stearnes, 1976). Differential maturation, mortality and regression may especially affect these results.

Interactions with Selection. When selection is nonrandom, many interactions (that is, differential effects for one group over another) may occur. Some examples are:

1. *Testing × selection:* Practice in test taking could affect some groups more than others. Testing is also a threat if different test forms or levels are used for the treatment and comparison groups (Wood, 1978).

2. *Instrumentation × selection:* A threat if groups are not measured at the same time.

3. *Maturation × selection:* The two groups may not mature at the same rate, and therefore the comparison group scores would not yield a good no-treatment expectation for the Title I students.

4. *Regression × selection:* Differential regression (Tallmadge and Wood, 1976) can occur if students are selected to be Title I or the comparison group in different schools or classes based on a common cut-off percentile. One group may be farther from the mean of its population than the other and hence will tend to regress more.

5. *History × selection:* It is very difficult to ensure that students in the comparison and Title I groups receive exactly the same educational experiences except for the Title I project.

Model C: Threats to Internal Validity

Model C, the regression model, uses a group of students scoring higher than the treatment students on the pretest as the comparison students. It is assumed that without treatment the Title I students would retain their *relative position* with respect to the comparison students and hence would have scores that would tend to lie on the same post-on-pretest regression line as that for the comparison group. Any difference between the post-on-pretest regression lines for the Title I and comparison students would be a measure of program impact.

Model C, the special regression model, requires that students be selected into the Title I program on the basis of a designated covariate *only*. The covariate can be a single variable such as a pretest or a composite score based on two or more variables. Under the assumption that comparison group students and selected Title I students are members of a single population, a linear regression equation predicting posttest scores from the covariate is derived from comparison group students who have not received supplemental services. This regression equation is applied to the Title I group. The result is a predicted posttest score (that is, a no-treatment expectation) for the Title I group.

Several studies have shown that if the assumptions of the model hold, unbiased estimates of the no-treatment-expectation results (Long, Horwitz, and Pellegrini, 1979; Stewart, 1980; Yap, 1979). An unbiased estimate means that using the model in situations having no treatment yields a project gain of zero on the average. That is, any single result may differ from zero but overall, the result is zero.

Two problems arise. The first is that the assumptions of the model may be difficult to satisfy in many cases. Model C is very sensitive to violations of the assumption of linearity (Stewart, 1980). Nonparallel regression lines between the Title I and comparison groups can result from numerous causes—ceiling or floor effects, invalid test scores, and differential project effects in Title I students to name a few. The kind of data snooping necessary to determine the reliability of Model C in a particular case may be too difficult for many LEAs (Boruch and DeGracie, 1977).

The second problem is that even though the estimate of project effect is unbiased on the average, it can still be misleading in any single evaluation. This can happen especially if the correlation between the pretest and posttest is small (perhaps below .75). Yap (1979) has shown that, with low correlations, no-treatment expectations can be off by over 10 NCEs.

The following discussion of threats to validity bear on two topics—factors related to nonlinearity and other factors that can yield alternative explanations of results.

Maturation. The posttest-on-pretest linear regression takes into account changes in the general level of performance from the pretest to the posttest. It is in this way that general maturation is controlled in Model C. Selection × maturation interactions, as discussed under interactions with selection, can pose a threat, however.

Instrumentation. Floor and ceiling effects can affect the regression lines used to estimate the no-treatment expectation (Estes and Anderson, 1978; Boruch and DeGracie, 1977). In order to convert evaluation results to NCEs in Model C2, the standard deviation of the national population must be estimated using the ratio of standard deviations of the treatment group on the normed and nonnormed tests.

Statistical Regression. Model C requires that Title I students be selected only on the pretest or a composite score. The process for selection is determined and the effects of regression are taken into account in the analyses.

Selection. Even though students of different ability are in the treatment and comparison groups, effects of these prior differences are controlled by selection on a covariate that assumes comparison groups and the Title I group are drawn from a single population and that the relationship between the covariate and the posttest is linear.

Mortality. Model C requires that both pretest (or a composite score) and posttest scores are available to complete the analysis. Students who drop out of either the treatment group or the comparison group could effect the results of a Model C analysis.

Interactions with Selection. The possible interactions that could pose threats to the internal validity of Model C include selection × maturation, selection × testing, selection × statistical regression, and selection × mortality. These could result in nonlinear or heterogeneous regression which would seriously affect the usefulness of the model.

Other. *Diffusion or imitation of the treatment, compensatory equalization of the treatment, compensatory rivalry* and *resentful demoralization of respondents using less desirable treatments.* All of these are more possible in Model C than in Model A since comparison groups are local. Whether or not they occur is a function of how the model is implemented.

Summary

Development and dissemination of the TIERS has prompted considerable commentary on its technical soundness. Hundreds of papers (many of them unpublished) have examined technical issues thought to bear on the soundness of the TIERS. The authors provided an overview of the threats to internal validity associated with each of the TIERS evaluation models by summarizing findings and conclusions of papers bearing on each threat to internal validity for each model. In short, a familiar conceptual framework was applied to facilitate a research based analysis of the TIERS.

It is apparent that Model A is theoretically vulnerable to threats due to maturation, instrumentation, statistical regression, and various interactions with selection. Model A, however, is quite easy to implement compared to Models B and C. Taking care to insure that each application satisfies the assumptions of Model A should reduce the effect of these threats.

Model B is relatively free from threats to internal validity unless it is not properly implemented. The major factor contributing to poor implementation is the failure to randomly assign students.

The greatest difficulty with Model C appears to be the risk of nonlinear regression of the posttest on the measure used for selection. Threats to validity that may contribute to nonlinear regression include selection × maturation interactions and instrumentation (floor and ceiling effects).

It is clear that none of the Title I Evaluation and Reporting System evaluation models is without threats to validity. Models B and C are theoretically rigorous but are difficult to implement. Model A is subject to a number of theoretical problems, but may be useful if data checks are used. Indeed, the most important aspect when using any of the models is not the inherent worth of the model itself, but the care that is taken when designing the evaluation, analyzing the data, and interpreting the results.

References

Armor, D., Conry-Oseguera, P., Cox, M., King, N., McDonnell, L., Pascal, A., Pauly, E., and Zellman, G. *Analysis of the School Preferred Reading Program in Selected Los Angeles Minority Schools.* Report prepared for the Los Angeles Unified School District, R-2007-LAUSD. Santa Monica, Calif.: Rand Corporation, 1976.

Arter, J. A., and Estes, G. D. "A Model for Developing Local Norms With a Standardized Achievement Measure for Use With Local Program Evaluation." Paper presented at annual American Educational Research Association meeting, Toronto, 1978.

Baker, R., and Williams, T. "Issues Related to Interpolation." National Testing Service, Technical Assistance Center, 1978.

Boruch, R. F., and DeGracie, J. S. "The Use of Regression Discontinuity Model With Criterion-Referenced Testing on the Evaluation of Compensatory Education." Paper presented at annual American Educational Research Association meeting, New York, 1977.

Bridgemann, B. "Extrapolation and Interpolation in Model A1 Title I Evaluation." Educational Testing Service, 1978.

Burton, B. "Longitudinal Norm-Referenced Evaluation: The Search for a Model." Paper presented at annual American Educational Research Association meeting, San Francisco, 1979.

Campbell, D. T., and Stanley, J. C. *Experimental and Quasi-Experimental Designs for Research.* Chicago: Rand McNally, 1966.

Coleman, J. S., Campbell, E. Q., Hobson, C. J., McPartland, J., Mood, A. M., Weinfeld, F. D., and York, R. L. *Equality of Educational Opportunity.* U.S Department of Health, Education and Welfare, Office of Education. Washington, D.C.: Government Printing Office, 1966.

Conklin, J. E., Burstein, L., and Keesling, J. W. "The Effects of Date of Testing and Method of Interpolation On the Use of Standardized Test Scores On the Evaluation of Large-Scale Educational Programs." *Journal of Educational Measurement,* 1979, *16,* 239–246.

Cook, T. D., and Campbell, D. T. "The Design and Conduct of Quasi-Experiments and True Experiments in Field Settings." In M. D. Dunnette (Ed.), *Handbook of Industrial and Organizational Psychology.* Chicago: Rand McNally, 1976.

Crane, L. R., and Cech, J. "Title I Evaluation Models A1 and B1: An Empirical Comparison." Paper presented at annual American Educational Research Association meeting, San Francisco, 1979.

Cronbach, L. J., Rogosa, D. R., Ploden, R. E., and Price, G. G. "Analysis of Covariance in Nonrandomized Experiments: Parameters Affecting Bias." Occasional paper, Stanford Evaluation Consortium, 1976.

Crowder, C. R. "Relation of Out-of-Level Testing to Ceiling and Floor Effects On Third- and Fifth-Grade Students." Paper presented at annual American Educational Research Association meeting, Toronto, 1978.

David, J. L., and Pelavin, S. H. "Evaluating Compensatory Education: Over What Period of Time Should Achievement Be Measured?" *Journal of Educational Measurement,* 1978, *15,* 91–99.

DeVito, P. J., and Long, J. V. "The Effects of Spring-Spring vs. Fall-Spring Testing Upon the Evaluation of Compensatory Education Programs." Paper presented at the annual American Educational Research Association meeting, New York, 1977.

Doherty, W. *Restandardization Study.* Santa Monica, Calif.: System Development Corp., 1976.

Echternacht, G. "A Note on Selection and the Norm-Referenced Model." Princeton, N.J.: Educational Testing Service, 1978.

ESEA Title I Annual Evaluation Report: FY 1975. Columbia, S.C.: Office of Federal Programs, South Carolina Department of Education, November 1975.

Estes, G. D., and Anderson, J. I. "Observed Treatment Effects With Special Regression Evaluation Models in Groups With No Treatment." Paper presented at annual American Educational Research Association meeting, Toronto, 1978.

Faddis, B. J., and Arter, J. A. "An Empirical Comparison of ESEA Title I Models A and B." Paper presented at annual American Educational Research Association meeting, San Francisco, 1979.

Faddis, B. J., and Estes, G. D. "Fall-to-Spring versus Fall-to-Fall Evaluations of a Large Title I Program With a Comparison Group Design." Paper presented at annual American Educational Research Association meeting, Toronto, 1978.

Fishbein, R. L. "The Use of Nonnormed Tests in the ESEA Title I Evaluation and Reporting System—Some Technical and Policy Issues." Paper presented at annual American Educational Research Association meeting, Toronto, 1978.

Friendly, L. P. "Changing Test Forms on Title I Evaluation." Unpublished manuscript. Mountain View, Calif.: RMC Research Corp., 1980.

Fuentes, E. J., and Jeffress, E. L. "The Use of Teacher Estimates of Children's Achievement In Selecting Appropriate Test Levels Versus Blanket Out-of-Level Testing: The Problem of an Efficient Method of Matching the Student's Functional Level With the Proper Test Level." Center for Educational Research and Evaluation, Research Triangle Institute, Research Triangle Park, North Carolina. Paper presented at annual American Educational Research Association meeting, Toronto, 1978.

Glass, G. *Regression Effect.* Memorandum, March 8, 1978.

Goldberger, A. S. *Selection Bias in Evaluating Treatment Effects: Some Formal Illustrations.* Institute for Research on Poverty, Discussion Papers. Madison: University of Wisconsin, 1972.

Haenn, J. F., and Proctor, D. C. "A Practitioner's Guide to Out-of-Level Testing." Paper presented at annual American Educational Research Association meeting, Toronto, 1978.

Hammond, D. C., Hepworth, D. H., and Smith, V. G. *Improving Therapeutic Communication: A Guide for Developing Effective Techniques.* San Francisco: Jossey-Bass, 1977.

Hammond, P. A., and Frechtling, J. A. "Twelve-, Nine-, and Three-Month Achievement Gains of Low and Average Achieving Elementary School Students." Paper presented at annual American Educational Research Association meeting, San Francisco, 1979.

Hardy, R. A. "Comparison of Model A and Model C: Results of First-Year Implementation in Florida." Educational Testing Service, unpublished paper, January 1979.

Hiscox, S. B., and Owens, T. R. "Behind the Basic Assumption of Model A." Paper presented at annual American Educational Research Association meeting, Toronto, 1978.

Holthouse, N. D., Stofflet, F. P., and Tokar, E. B. *Achievement, Social Class, and the Summer Vacation.* Norfolk, Va.: Norfolk Public Schools, 1976.

House, G. D. "A Comparison of Title I Achievement Results Obtained Under USOE Models A1, C1 and a Mixed Model." Paper presented at annual American Educational Research Association meeting, San Francisco, 1979.

Jaeger, R. M. "On Combining Achievement Test Data Through the NCE Scaled Score." Paper presented at annual Conference of Directors of State Testing Programs, Princeton, N.J., 1978.

Kaskowitz, D. H. *The Effect of Attrition on the Title I Evaluation and Reporting Systems.* Mountain View, Calif.: RMC Research Corp., 1980.

Kaskowitz, D. H., and Norwood, C. R. *A Study of the Norm-Referenced Procedure for Evaluating Project Effectiveness as Applied in the Evaluation of Project Information Packages.* Stanford Research Institute Research Memorandum URU-3556. Menlo Park, Calif.: Stanford Research Institute, 1977.

Klibanoff, L. S. *The Adequacy of the Formula Used to Estimate the Population Standard Deviation of Nonnormed Tests.* Mountain View, Calif.: RMC Research Corp., 1980.

Linn, R. L. "Evaluation of Title I via the RMC Models: A Critical Review." Paper presented at CSE Invitational Conference on Measurement and Methodology, Center for the Study of Evaluation, UCLA, Los Angeles, January 4-5, 1978.

Long, J., Horwitz, S., and DeVito, P. "An Empirical Investigation of the ESEA Title I Evaluation System's Proposed Variance Estimation Procedure for Use With Criterion-Referenced Tests." Paper presented at annual American Educational Research Association meeting, Toronto, 1978.

Long, J., Horwitz, S., and Pellegrini, A. "An Empirical Investigation of the ESEA Title I Evaluation System's No-Treatment Expectation for the Special Regression Model (C1)." Paper presented at annual American Educational Research Association meeting, San Francisco, 1979.

Long, J. V., Schaffran, J. A., and Kellogg, T. M. "Effects of Out-of-Level Survey Testing on Reading Achievement Scores of Title I, ESEA Students." *Journal of Educational Measurement,* 1977, *14,* 203-213.

Mandeville, G. K. "An Evaluation of Title I Model C1: The Special Regression Model." Paper presented at annual American Educational Research Association meeting, Toronto, 1978.

Mayeske, G. W., and Beaton, A., Jr. *Special Studies of Our Nation's Students.* Washington, D.C.: Government Printing Office, 1975.

Murray, S. L. "An Analysis of Regression Effects and the Equipercentile Growth Assumption in the Norm-Referenced Evaluation Model." Paper presented at the Washington Educational Research Association Meeting, Seattle, 1978.

Murray, S. L. "An Architect Looks at Alternative Plans." Paper presented at annual American Educational Research Association meeting, San Francisco, 1979.

Murray, S. L., Arter, J., and Faddis, B. "Title I Technical Issues As Threats to Internal Validity of Experimental and Quasi-Experimental Designs." Paper presented at annual American Educational Research Association meeting, San Francisco, 1979.

Norwood, C. R., and Stearnes, M. *Evaluation of the Field Test of Project Information Packages.* Menlo Park, Calif.: Stanford Research Institute, 1976.

Ozenne, A. "The Effect of Vertical-Scaling Imprecision in the Estimation of Title I Project Gains." Paper presented at annual American Educational Research Association meeting, Toronto, 1978.

Pellegrini, A., Horwitz, S., and Long, J. "An Empirical Investigation of the ESEA Title I Evaluation System's Proposed Variance Estimation Procedures and the Proposed Alternative for Estimation (sic) Variances in Title I Evaluation Models for Use With Criterion Referenced Tests." Paper presented at annual American Educational Research Association meeting, San Francisco, 1979.

Powers, S. "Implications of Out-of-Level Testing for ESEA Title I Students." Paper presented at annual American Educational Research Association meeting, Toronto, 1978.

Powell, G., Schmidt, J., and Raffeld, P. "The Equipercentile Assumption as a Pseudo-Control Group Estimate of Gain." Paper presented at annual American Educational Research Association meeting, San Francisco, 1979.

Powers, S. "A Comparison of ESEA Title I Student Gains in a Fall-Spring and Fall-Fall Out-of-Level Testing Schedule." Paper presented at annual American Educational Research Association meeting, San Francisco, 1979.

Roberts, S. J. *Cognitive Growth Over the Summer.* Mountain View, Calif.: RMC Research Corp., 1980.

Roberts, O. A. *Regression to the Mean and the Regression-Effect Bias.* Mountain View, Calif.: RMC Research Corp., 1980a.

Roberts, O. A. *Practice Effect on Test Wiseness.* Mountain View, Calif.: RMC Research Corp., 1980b.

Scherich, H. *A Case for Instructionally Dated Norms.* Durham, N.C.: NTS Research Corp., 1978.

Slaughter, H. B., and Gallas, E. J. "Will Out-of-Level Norm-Referenced Testing Improve the Selection of Program Participants and the Diagnosis of Reading Comprehension in ESEA Title I Programs?" Paper presented at annual American Educational Research Association meeting, Toronto, 1978.

Slinde, J. A., and Linn, R. L. "Vertically Equated Tests: Fact or Phantom?" *Journal of Educational Measurement,* 1977, *14,* 23–32.

Stammon, D., Raffeld, P., and Powell, G. "A Simulation Study of the Effectiveness of Two Estimates of Regression on the Title I Model A Procedure." Paper presented at annual American Educational Research Association meeting, San Francisco, 1979.

Stenner, A. J., and Bland, J. D. "Assumptions about Summer Growth Implicit in Norm-Referenced Achievement Tests." Durham, N.C.: NTS Research Corp., 1979.

Stenner, A. J., Hunter, E. L., Bland, J. D., and Cooper, M. L. "The Standardized Growth Expectation: Implications for Educational Evaluation." Paper presented at annual American Educational Research Association meeting, Toronto, 1978.

Stewart, B. L. *The Regression Model on Title I Evaluation.* Mountain View, Calif.: RMC Research Corp., 1980.

Stewart, B. L., and Tallmadge, G. K. "Interlevel Articulation and Title I Evaluation." Paper presented at annual American Educational Research Association meeting, Boston, 1980.

Storlie, T. R., Rice, W., Harvey, P., and Crane, L. R. "An Empirical Comparison of Title I NCE Gains Estimated With Model A1 and With Model A2." Paper presented at annual American Educational Research Association meeting, San Francisco, 1979.

Storlie, T. R., Rice, W., Johnson, M. L., and Crowe, M. B. "Local Norms in a Large Urban Setting for Evaluating Title I Programs with Model A1." Paper presented at annual American Educational Research Association meeting, San Francisco, 1979.

Tallmadge, G. K., and Horst, D. P. "The Use of Different Achievement Tests in ESEA Title I Evaluation System." Paper presented at annual American Educational Research Association meeting, Toronto, 1978.

Tallmadge, G. K., and Wood, C. T. *User's Guide: ESEA Title I Evaluation and Reporting System.* Mountain View, Calif.: RMC Research Corp., 1976.

Thistlethwaite, D. L., and Campbell, D. T. "Regression-Discontinuity Analysis: An Alternative to the Ex Post Facto Experiment." *Journal of Educational Psychology,* 1960.

Wood, C. T. "Norming Practices and the Norm-Referenced Evaluation Model." In B. L. Bessey (Ed.), *Further Documentation of State ESEA Title I Reporting Models and Their Technical Assistance Requirements.* Phase II, Volume 2. Mountain View, Calif.: RMC Research Corporation, 1978.

Wood, C. T. *The Adequacy of the Equipercentile Assumption in the Norm-Referenced Evaluation Model.* Mountain View, Calif.: RMC Research Corp., 1980a.

Wood, C. T. *A Summary of the Phase I Analyses of the Technical Evaluation Issues.* Mountain View, Calif.: RMC Research Corp., 1980b.

Yap, K. O. "Can Selection Tests Be Used As Pretests?" Paper presented at annual American Educational Research Association meeting, Toronto, 1978.

Yap, K. O. "Pretest-Posttest Correlation and Regression Models." Paper presented at annual American Educational Research Association meeting, San Francisco, 1979.

Steve Murray and Judy Arter are consultants with the Title I Technical Assistance Centers for HEW Regions 8, 9, and 10 at the Northwest Regional Educational Laboratory in Portland, Oregon.

Functional-level testing is fundamental to the evaluation models,
although criteria for determining what is a functional-level test
are unclear. Reliability and validity of test scores
in the range of chance is at issue.

Toward Functional Criteria for Functional-Level Testing in Title I Evaluation

Kenneth M. Wilson
Thomas F. Donlon

Title I funded compensatory education projects in grades two through twelve that are concerned with the improvement of basic skills in reading, other English language arts, or mathematics must be evaluated according to one of three standard evaluation models, or approved alternatives, that have been developed for use by local educational agencies (LEAs or school districts), as described in detail elsewhere (Tallmadge and Wood, 1978). Though differing in detail, the models have certain features in common, including, for example:

1. use of systematic and equitable procedures for selecting pupils who will receive services (called treatment groups).
2. pretesting toward the beginning and posttesting toward the end of each project.
3. estimating project gain, defined as the difference between the observed posttest standing of a treatment group and a model-unique estimate of expected standing in the absence of treatment (called a "no-treatment expectation").

By far the most popular model is the so-called norm-referenced model, or Model A1, which according to some estimates (for example, Echternacht, 1978), is being employed in more than 75 and possibly up to 99 percent of all local evaluations.

Implementation of Model A1 calls for preselection of participants (typically in the spring), pretesting them in the fall and posttesting them in the following spring. Use of the same test (form and level) is recommended. Assessment of project gain is based on what has been termed the "equipercentile assumption is not an issue in this chapter. It is conditioned upon a requirement that project participants be selected before they are pretested, a step which is to the national normative group from pretest to posttest. (The validity of this assumption is not as issue in this chapter. It is conditioned upon a requirement that project participants be selected before they are pretested, a step which is assumed to introduce a correction for regression.) For example, if the fall pretest standing of Title I third graders is at the fifteenth centile relative to empirical fall norms for third graders nationally, it is assumed that the posttest average on the test would be at the fifteenth centile level relative to empirical spring norms for third graders in the absence of any Title I services. Any improvement in centile standing (translated into Normal Curve Equivalents or NCEs) is defined as project gain. All group standings must be referenced to national norms for age/grade peers of the Title I group. Hence use of nationally normed standardized tests is emphasized.

In connection with all the models, emphasis has been placed on the use of appropriate measures. Model users are given wide latitude to select tests that meet general technical standards of reliability and validity. However, especially in connection with the norm-referenced model, emphasis has been placed on what has been termed "functional level tests"—that is, tests whose content is consistent with the objectives of a Title I project concerned with improvement of basic skills and whose difficulty level corresponds to the "functional" (performance, instructional) level of the Title I pupils.

Model developers (RMC) and Technical Assistance Centers (TACs) have provided through printed materials, workshops, and other means a variety of guidelines for determining whether a given test is a functional-level test for a given group of pupils. *It is a basic thesis of this chapter that current guidelines should be strengthened.* This thesis is developed within the framework of the following interrelated themes and arguments, each of which is elaborated briefly in the body of the chapter:

(1) Current guidelines for functional-level testing, especially with respect to assessing the appropriate difficulty level of a test for a group, raise questions regarding the appropriateness of in-level achievement testing, since in many Title I settings an in-level test may generate a score distribution centered near its chance-level floor. To avoid interpretive ambiguities associated with scores in the chance range, evaluators are instructed to test out-of-level.

(2) Due to weaknesses in the existing measurement "system," especially increasingly well-documented limitations of interlevel articulation through vertical equating, referencing out-of-level to in-level performance introduces its own set of interpretive ambiguities—ambiguities that do not appear to be amenable to clarification or assessment through empirical procedures likely to be applicable in local settings.

(3) Current guidelines tacitly encourage inferences regarding lack of measurement utility in chance-level scores based on implicit assumptions (of

excessive randomness, hence unreliability, hence invalidity) that are capable of empirical verification. Moreover, direct evidence of significant measurement utility (for example, predictive and concurrent validity) for chance-level scores has been found in a number of operational settings, and evidence of the nonrandom properties of such scores (hence some potential for measurement utility) has been adduced in a relatively large number of studies. Thus, there is reason to believe that low scores generated by in-level testing in Title I settings may have a sufficient degree of validity and reliability for purposes of assessing group gains in norm-referenced evaluation.

(4) Certain of the methods that can be used to test the assumption of "randomness" in observed chance-level scores, especially correlational methods involved in assessing predictive or concurrent validity, are highly relevant for all evaluation models, and it is important that all local evaluators become familiar with correlational concepts and methods.

(5) Current guidelines appear to be too conservative. They reject in-level scores on rough criteria that do not help evaluators differentiate between chance-level bath water and measurement baby. Appropriately strengthened guidelines should encourage local evaluators to employ approaches and methods designed to help clarify recognized interpretive ambiguities associated with the use of tests that are of above average difficulty for a group, by demonstrating whether or not the scores generated by that test have the basic measurement properties needed to warrant their use in assessing group gains within the framework of the norm-referenced model, namely, validity and reliability.

(6) Test publishers can and should reinforce such guidelines by providing services or conducting research designed to clarify questions regarding the measurement properties of scores in the chance-range and by alerting test users generally to the interpretive ambiguities associated with treating as comparable scores on *different* tests, which have been designed for populations at different educational levels, which differ intentionally in the difficulty levels of the items involved, and which necessarily differ somewhat in content.

Current Guidelines

With respect to test content, evaluators have been encouraged to make systematic comparisons of the test items with instructional materials and stated objectives of instruction. A test that exhibits a "satisfactory" degree of agreement may be either an in-level test (that is, one standardized on a national sample at the same grade placement as that of the Title I pupils) or an out-of-level test (for example, one standardized for use at a lower grade level). Since Title I pupils may be receiving instruction at grade level in their regular classroom program and at a lower level in their Title I program, there are elements of ambiguity involved in deciding which set of (presumably) related curricular objectives should be considered paramount, and both the in-level and the out-of-level test may include a partially representative set of items.

With respect to *test difficulty*, emphasis has been placed on identifying characteristics or conditions conducive to maximum efficiency of measurement (high reliability) within a given group.

It has been noted, for example, that the highest reliability of a test is achieved when the students on the average get slightly more than half the items correct; and it has been suggested (for example, by Roberts, 1976) that a test is most suitable for a given group when the mean raw score of the group is equal to or above a third of the maximum score and somewhat less than three-fourths of the maximum (implicitly assuming four choices per question).

For determining whether a given test is "too difficult" for a group, particular emphasis has been placed on procedures for detecting "floor effects" which are said to be present when individuals begin to score within the range which could be attained by chance (see Roberts, 1978). (Throughout this chapter emphasis is placed on the problems associated with evaluations involving "low-scoring" individuals. Problems involved with a test that is much "too easy" for a group are recognized but are not especially critical in Title I evaluation settings. And, in general, "ceiling" effects are much less ambiguous than "floor effects.") It is reasoned that the scores of individuals as well as the mean scores at levels that could have been attained by chance (guessing) are likely to be artificially inflated, and hence to overestimate the true level of performance. Moreover, it is assumed that in groups where floor effects are indicated (by high concentrations of scores in the chance-score range), the reliability of measurement is likely to be attenuated.

Generalized rules of thumb have been suggested for identifying that point in a raw score distribution at which floor effects may become important, such as the following (Roberts, 1978): Given a test composed of n-choice items, the floor may be determined by using the formula $[1/(n-1)] \times$ number of items. (Other indications of floor effects are said to include the presence of positive skewness in the raw score distribution [Roberts, 1978, pp. 5–7]. It is interesting to note that if the raw score distribution on a multiple choice test for a given group is due solely to random marking of answer sheets [is solely a function of chance], the distribution of scores would be expected to be symmetrical, not skewed. A comparison of a distribution of observed scores in the chance-score range and a computer-generated set of random scores is provided below.)

Generalized guidelines such as the foregoing are derived from the assumption of test-score "noninterpretability" below that point in the score distribution specified by the mean chance-score plus two chance-score standard deviations, as enunciated by testing authorities.

Gulliksen (1950), for example, asserted that scores "within one or two standard deviations of a chance score should not be interpreted as signifying any knowledge of the subject matter of the examinations" (p. 263). To avoid the ambiguities involved in observed chance-level scores, Guilford (1950, p. 448) suggested the desirability of keeping "a multiple choice test so easy that not only chance scores are avoided but also those within two standard errors of mean chance expectation."

It has been noted that the presence of floor effects is only suggestive of the possibility that the test involved is "too difficult" for a group. However, the guidelines presented have tended to suggest implicitly that if "floor effects" are detected, then the test is not "appropriate" for the purpose of assessing project gain.

If current guidelines are applied to the analyses of the score distributions of pupils in publisher's national normative samples, significant proportions of these pupils, tested in-level, appear to be earning scores of questionable utility. Roberts (1978), for example, using the general rules for determining floor effects as the basis for identifying the questionable score level, reported corresponding floor percentiles for eight widely used reading and mathematics tests for grades two through six. For the reading tests, most of the floor-level percentiles were at or above the tenth percentile and for about half of all the subtests surveyed in this way, the floor began at or above the twentieth percentile. Trends for mathematics tests were similar.

Hopkins (1964) earlier called attention to a similar pattern after examining twenty-eight subtests from four well-known achievement batteries. For the twenty-eight subtests he determined, among other things, the percentage of the normative samples with scores whose interpretability was questionable according to the "mean chance plus two standard errors" rule. The median percentage with questionable scores ranged from forty-eight percent (at grade four) to sixteen percent (at grade six).

Most Title I participants will be performing (functioning) at levels that are below average for their grade-placement. In many districts, Title I pupils will earn scores averaging at or below percentile levels such as those cited above for in-level tests. An in-level test clearly is not likely to be of "average difficulty" for Title I pupils in most districts and the scores for Title I pupils tested in-level will be in the "questionable" difficulty range according to current guidelines. Thus, current guidelines for identifying a functional-level test tend to raise questions regarding the appropriateness of in-level testing.

Out-of-Level Testing: A Flawed Solution

If the in-level test is judged to be "too difficult" to be considered a functional-level test for purposes of Title I evaluation, the primary option available is to test out-of-level—that is, to use an easier test level, designed for pupils in a lower grade than that of the pupils in the project. For example, for pupils in a fourth-grade Title I mathematics project, a publisher's test level standardized and normed for use at the third grade level could be considered. The easier test might be closer in content to the instruction being given to the low-achieving fourth graders in their Title I project than the recommended in-level fourth-grade test. If so, use of the easier test should result in somewhat more reliable measurement of differences in math performance *among members of the low performing fourth-grade group* than would have been obtained with the in-level test.

However, the comparisons of greatest interest where fourth graders are concerned tend to involve other fourth graders. And, one of the critical requirements in Title I evaluation is that regardless of the test level administered, performance on the test must be translated into in-level percentiles. Thus, if Title I (or other) fourth graders are tested with a third-grade-level test, their scores must be referenced to empirical norms for fourth graders.

Such cross-level referencing is possible in multilevel test series in which scores on the successive levels have been linked or vertically equated to a common, standard-score scale, using one of several available models for equating tests assumed to be measuring the same function but at different levels of difficulty (see Angoff, 1971, for a detailed discussion of various equating models, problems, and issues). Vertically equated scales are generally referred to as expanded standard-score scales.

From the point of view of the practitioner, the process of converting scores on an out-of-level test to estimated in-level scores is not unduly complicated and simply requires attention to the score-conversion sequence characteristic of a given test series, using conversion tables provided by a publisher. *However, the ease with which scores may be converted belies the interpretive complications that are introduced when scores on one test level are used as "surrogates" for scores on another.* In situations involving off-level testing which call for or require in-level norm referencing, or comparisons of groups or individuals who have taken different test levels, the extent to which scores obtained through the conversion process are "equivalent" becomes the most important consideration.

Are "equivalent" scores equivalent? Setting aside important questions regarding a basic assumption of vertical equating—namely that the same function is being measured across several successive achievement test levels that are grade-referenced in respect to content in arithmetic, reading, or language skills—the critical issue with respect to the out-of-level to in-level conversion requirement is one of accuracy—that is, are scores earned on one test level and their estimated equivalents on another test level actually "equivalent"? If adjacent (or more discrepant) test levels are administered to students in the same grade, will each student's raw score yield essentially the same expanded-scale score and the same percentile rank with respect to grade-level norms regardless of test level taken? Are the discrepancies between converted and observed scores systematic or variable with respect to magnitude and direction across levels, grade or ability groups, or test series?

There is a growing body of evidence, most of it recent, bearing on these important questions. Generally speaking, results of studies of the accuracy of vertical equating across test levels indicate that there are discrepancies of practical significance associated with the estimation of scores on one test level from scores obtained on another level, regardless of the test series, test levels, grade or ability groups, and method of equating. Such evidence has been found in research involving the examination of test data generated in large-scale equating, normative, or evaluation studies, and in a small number of studies involving data from operational testing programs at local levels. Salient characteristics of the research evidence are highlighted in the summary which follows.

In a reexamination of selected test data from the Anchor Test Study [ATS] (Loret, Seder, Bianchini, and Vale, 1972), Linn (1975) and Slinde and Linn (1977) found discrepancies between in-grade and estimated in-grade scores that were not consistent across tests, test levels, or score distributions—differences that were judged to be large enough to have a significant impact on an observed outcome. (For example, as Slinde and Linn observed, "several of these differences are as large as a third of a [within-grade] standard deviation, and a difference this big is apt to loom large relative to the magnitude of the 'effects' being investigated" (1977, p. 26). Their study employed the equipercentile method of equating two adjacent levels of one test (the MAT) via a third, base test (the CAT). Noting that other methods of equating (for example,) methods based on item-characteristics curve theory, after Lord, (1977), might lead to more satisfactory interlevel articulation, Slinde and Linn (1978, 1979) in two later studies explored the utility of the Rasch model (as described, for example, by Wright, 1977) in two quite different data contexts for calibrating scores on easy and difficult tests. Results indicated that the problem of interlevel articulation was not resolved (in the data contexts involved) within the framework of the model employed.

In a more recent study employing the Rasch model with data from three overlapping levels of the Iowa Tests of Basic Skills, mathematics computation subtests with samples of sixth-, seventh-, and eighth-grade students in Iowa, Loyd and Hoover (1980, p. 188) concluded as did Slinde and Linn (1978, pp. 33–34) that the application to one group of ability estimates obtained from a different group did not seem to provide the equivalent measurements that are necessary for longitudinal research. Other equating methods were also applied to the data with results indicating significant differences in results associated with method. (In assessing results using the Rasch model, these investigators examined the assumption of unidimensionality—that is, that a single trait is being assessed by several successive levels of a given test—and concluded on the basis of factor analytic results that that assumption was not strictly met in the data under consideration. They suggested that performance on different math-test levels may be a function of the pattern of introduction into the curriculum of different sets of skills at certain grade levels.)

In an actual operational setting, low-achieving students in Rhode Island were administered both in- and out-of-level versions of the Gates McGinnitie reading tests. Long, Schaffran, and Kellogg (1977) found that lower-level tests consistently underestimated performance on the in-level test for second and third graders, while opposite results obtained for fourth graders; in a subsequent, related study with the same test, Long (1979) used out-of-level norms tables provided by the publisher and found continued systematic differences between standard scores estimated from in-level and below-level tests administered to the same students, most of which were statistically significant.

Comparable results have been reported by Doherty (1977), who found that when two nominally appropriate adjacent levels of the CAT were administered to fourth graders, percentile ranks estimated by the two measures differed considerably, and by Pelavin and Barker (1976), who found that grade-level versions of the MAT consistently produced higher estimates of reading performance than lower levels in grades four through nine.

One of the most thorough critiques of the problems of interlevel articulation has been provided recently by Stewart (1980), who examined much of the evidence cited here and reported the results of his own comprehensive study of the accuracy of interlevel articulation in two large data bases. Stewart found significant anomalies associated with vertical equating analyses of performance on adjacent test levels of two widely used series.

Stewart and other investigators have found significant discrepancies associated with score conversions via vertically equated scales when the test levels involved are adjacent. There is reason to believe that the psychometric soundness and the conceptual tenability of linking different test levels to a common-scale decrease significantly as the distance between test levels increases. In commenting on the design of his own investigation of interlevel articulation, which involved adjacent levels only, Stewart (1980, p. 4) noted that although in principle vertical equating may span more than a single adjacent test level, estimates of in-level scores derived from performance on more distant test levels are likely to be both inaccurate and misleading. Tests differing by two or more levels are likely to include substantially different content, suggesting that the assumption of a single underlying dimension on which expanded standard scores may be scaled is untenable.

The results reported by Slinde and Linn (1978, 1979) and by Loyd and Hoover (1980) in studies that involved groups rather widely separated in ability or grade level and tests differing rather widely in difficulty or content lend support to Stewart's observation. Empirical evidence from operational contexts in which students have been tested with widely separated test levels is limited. However, one investigation of the effects of off-level assignment in the Dallas Independent School District (Appelbaum, 1979) indicated that the severity of GE discrepancies associated with vertical-scale transformations did, in fact, increase with distance between levels.

On balance, it seems clear that results of research on interlevel articulation constitute a rather lengthy litany of potential problems associated with, and raise doubts about assumptions underlying, the practice of treating as comparable or "equivalent" scores converted across levels via expanded standard score-scales. The practice of using alternate or parallel forms of achievement tests in Model A1 has been *discouraged,* and use of the same form and level for pre- and posttest has been encouraged, due in part to a recognition of the problems involved in treating as equivalent the scores earned on two tests which have been designed to measure the *same* attribute at the *same* level for the *same* population. Clearly, the problem of vertical equating (which calls for converting to a common scale scores on forms of a test designed for populations at different educational levels, which differ intentionally in the difficulty levels of the items involved, and which necessarily differ somewhat in content) is "substantially more difficult and conceptually more hazardous than that of horizontal equating (of two parallel tests)" (Slinde and Linn, 1978).

From the point of view of testing practice, especially but certainly not exclusively in connection with Title I evaluation, the available evidence clearly justified Stewart's (1980) conclusion that "any assessments of student progress or program effectiveness are likely to be confounded with vertical equating problems when different test levels are used for evaluation." Those problems are likely to increase with the distance between levels employed. Moreover, the nature of the discrepancies involved in converting scores across levels does not seem to be consistent across different levels within a given test series, different grade or ability groups, or different test series, and results obtained with different methods of equating do not appear to be comparable. This means that it is not possible to formulate generalizations that might help the evaluator anticipate (hence make some appropriate adjustments for) the direction or magnitude of error that may be introduced when more than one test level is employed.

In assessing the implications of the problem of interlevel articulation for Title I evaluators, Stewart (1980, p. 23) emphasizes what may be termed the context-specific nature of questions about cross-level equating. In situations where out-of-level testing may be involved he advises that "local evaluators should examine the accuracy of the vertical equating *for the test levels to be administered* with special attention to any discrepancies at the lower percentiles"; and more generally, that "thorough examinations of the vertical equating and the *actual behavior of adjacent tests in use* are both necessary if scores on adjacent levels are to be interpreted meaningfully" [emphasis added]. The techniques for assessing the accuracy of vertical equating in actual use contexts, which Stewart suggests illustratively, are likely to be very difficult for local evaluators to employ.

Taking a Closer Look at the Guidelines

Current guidelines tacitly encourage an intuitively appealing inference that a test which generates a score distribution centered near its chance-level floor is, ipso facto, lacking in measurement properties essential for its use in norm-referenced evaluation. It is, however, important to recognize that such an inference rests on *testable* assumptions regarding the degree of randomness in chance-level score variance—for example, that observed scores tend to reflect largely guessing behavior and, because of an excessive amount of random variance, are too unreliable for meaningful interpretation in connection with either individual or group assessment.

This section presents evidence bearing on the assumption of "randomness" in chance-level scores that has been provided by studies designed either to assess directly the utility and interpretability of such scores in operational settings or to determine whether or not observed chance-level test data (for individuals or groups) exhibit properties specified by theory under the assumption of random marking of answer sheets. This evidence suggests that assumption of randomness in chance-level scores should not be accepted uncritically—there may be real measurement utility in such scores.

Review of the Literature

Assessments of randomness in individual or group test records have been undertaken for a variety of purposes and have employed a variety of techniques. The primary techniques considered to date are as follows:

1. *Correlational methods* for assessing concurrent or predictive validity by demonstrating meaningful correlation of chance-level scores with other tests, or with nontest criteria such as college grades;

2. *Distributional methods* for assessing the degree of fit between observed distributions of scores in the chance range (or of option-choices for particular

test items) and distributions specified by theory assuming totally random marking of answer sheets;

3. *Internal consistency methods* for assessing the degree of agreement (through correlational procedures) between an individual's pattern of success-failure across test items and group-determined success-failure patterns for the items. The third type of method capitalizes on the proposition that a purely random responder will succeed only on easy items as readily as on hard ones; when tested by one of several correlational methods, the value of the coefficient for a "random responder" will approximate zero.

The methods classified above as "correlational," are most "powerful" since they demonstrate directly the needed properties; the reliability and validity of the disputed chance-level scores are empirically established. The other methods permit inferences regarding the nonrandom characteristics of observed chance-level data but do not directly establish the basic measurement properties of the data. However, evidence suggesting the nonrandom nature of observed chance-level data, through distributional and internal consistency techniques, supplements and reinforces evidence of a more direct nature.

Evidence from Correlational Studies. Evidence of the reliability and validity of chance-level scores has been generated in several studies designed to demonstrate these qualities in specific practical settings. Boldt (1968), for example, assessed the concurrent validity of chance-level scores on tests resembling the College Board Scholastic Aptitude Test (SAT), in order to evaluate the practice of reporting scaled-score equivalents of raw scores in the chance range. He analyzed the regression of scores from a middle-difficulty test on scores for a very difficult test and found that while the slope of the regression was somewhat flatter in the chance region than in the nonchance region, evidence of a regular systematic relationship persisted for scores well below *mean* chance level. He concluded that "the study establishes clearly that chance level scores should not be assumed to arise from purely random processes" (Boldt, 1968, p. 58).

Similar results were secured by Cliff (1958) who studied the School and College Ability Tests (SCAT). Analyzing data for both verbal and mathematical material, she focussed on whether below-chance scores were similar to above-chance scores in their correlation with similar but independent tests, concluding that the below-chance scores were, in fact, basically similar to the above-chance scores in their properties.

Examples of studies concerned with the predictive validity of scores in or near the chance-score range are those of Hills and Gladney (1968) and Hills and Stanley (1970), both of which involved analyses of the correlation with college grades, of chance or near-chance scores on the SAT, in college settings in which very high proportions of students earned such scores. Hills and Gladney, among other things, correlated below-mean-chance SAT scores with the college grade point average. They reported that results of analysis of covariance tests "did not show that the regression lines (for grades on SAT scores) in the samples with chance-level scores were different from the regression lines in the above-chance samples." However, in their data, predictive validity in the sharply restricted range of SAT scores between 200 and 230 (that is, below mean chance) was weak. The later study by Hills and Stanley demonstrated quite significant predictive validity for SAT scores in similar groups, with mean SAT scores centered near the chance range and very large proportions of scores in the chance range. They did not restrict their analysis to below-mean-chance scorers only.

A somewhat related, but more theoretical study by Levine and Lord (1959) considered the discriminating power of tests at different score levels using information functions that described the error of measurement for each score level. Their results suggested that even on a "formula" scored test, the negative scores (indicating performance below mean chance expectancy) would likely still have validity, with a score of -7, for example, predictive of poorer criterion performance than a score of, say, -2.

Evidence from Distributional Studies. Examples of such studies are those by MacRae and Green (1971), and Pike and Flaugher (1970). MacRae and Green were concerned with questions regarding the properties of observed chance-level score distributions on the California Reading Test. Using familiar chi-square goodness-of-fit techniques they determined that the observed chance-level score distribution differed significantly from that specified by theory under the assumption of random marking of answer sheets.

Pike and Flaugher evaluated evidence of randomness in data for individual test items. Their study considered the responses of center-city students, whose scores were predominantly in the chance range and involved a comparison of the empirical distribution of wrong answers across options with the rectangular one which is expected on under the assumption of random responding to item options. They found somewhat more evidence of rectangularity in the responses of the center-city students than in the responses of (higher scoring) suburban students but, for both groups, the evidence suggested general tendencies toward nonrectangularity for most items, hence nonrandom properties.

Evidence from Internal-Consistency Assessments. The correlational and distributional approaches are evaluations of group data. Internal consistency approaches to demonstrating nonrandomness of responses consider the internal properties of an individual record. If the responses are random, they will be uncorrelated with item difficulty as determined by the group. A chance response is as likely to succeed on a difficult item as it is on an easy one. Such chance responses will show no correlation with group-determined indices of item difficulty.

Fowler (1954), who studied the correlation of individuals and groups, calling the technique an appraisal of "person conformity," found that scores in his distributions yielded high values for his index of person conformity, indicating that they were not random.

In an analogous study Donlon and Fischer (1968) used the biserial correlation coefficient to appraise individual-group similarity, calling their index the "personal biserial." They studied the properties of scores in the chance range, defined as all scores lower than two standard deviations above the mean chance score, an an African sample taking an American test, the Preliminary

Scholastic Aptitude Test, a combination of test and group which yielded large numbers of chance-level scores.

The personal biserials of individuals in the chance range were, for the most part, significantly greater than zero, indicating that, in general, these individuals succeeded on easy items and failed on difficult ones. The personal biserials of low-scoring subjects were very similar to those of higher-scoring subjects.

To demonstrate the general reliability of the index as an aspect of personal test performance, Donlon and Fischer cross-correlated the value of the index on the PSAT verbal with values on the PSAT-mathematical. The result was a low positive correlation, indicating that the index reflected stable elements of test performance. Further, they considered a combination of cross-test predictors, using verbal total score and verbal personal biserial to predict mathematical total score. This cross-test multiple correlation, using the personal biserials, was .35, higher than the zero-order correlation between verbal and mathematical, .28. This indicates that the interpretation of a given score in terms of its implications for a score on the other test, would vary depending on the personal biserial. At a given score level, persons with higher biserials would be predicted to do better on the other test.

Donlon and Rindler (1979) carried out an exploratory study of the personal biserial with candidates for the Graduate Record Examination. They considered the distribution of such indexes separately for low-scoring groups defined by sex and ethnic background. All groups were characterized by average biserials well above chance. Further, the personal biserials demonstrated correlational properties similar to those reported in Donlon and Fischer (1968). The principal findings of the study confirmed that chance-level scores that demonstrate nonrandomness by positive correlations with item difficulty will have characteristics similar to scores which are significantly greater than mean chance. (Some confirmation of this is provided in an exploratory study by Stamman (undated) in TAC Region VI, who applied a method very similar to that of Fowler (1954) or of Donlon and Fischer (1968) to identify individuals whose patterns of successes and failures reflected randomness.)

Thus studies involving correlational, distributional, and internal consistency approaches are all uniformly supportive of the view that chance-level scores should not be assumed to be "random events." (This chapter will not review the use of the more complex methods suggested by Levine and Rubin (1979), which determine the probability of the unique answer pattern in the light of the estimation of the examinee's score level. Several mathematical models have been suggested by these authors, including models that assume variations in candidate ability from item to item. Such models may be applied to the evaluation of chance scores, but they are used to test general aberration in candidate response patterns.)

A Title I Example

The evidence from studies outside the Title I context appears to warrant the conclusion that it is important to avoid uncritical acceptance of the chance-score-range noninterpretability dictum and an operational corollary, namely, that it is important to carry out an assessment of the randomness assumption before abandoning a test which generates a large number of scores near its chance-level floor.

Results of one such assessment involving operational data from a fourth-grade Title I reading project serve, illustratively, to reinforce these conclusions. The data were gathered in implementing Model A-1, using the Metropolitan Achievement Test Elementary, Form F (1970), which is in-level for both the beginning and the end of grade four. The test has ninety-five four-chance items; mean chance is approximately 23.8, and chance standard deviation is approximately 4.2.

On the pretest, the raw score mean was 25.5, not far from the theoretical mean-chance level; moreover, fully 80 percent of the pupils scored below the level of "noninterpretability" suggested by Gulliksen (1950)—that is, mean chance plus two chance-score standard deviations, or in this case a raw score of .32.

As shown in Figure 1, however, for this group the pretest scores were systematically related to posttest scores (even though on the posttest about half the raw scores still fell below the "critical" level). Moreover, it is apparent that the pretest raw-score standard deviation (8.3) is considerably greater than that expected by chance (that is, 4.2), had the scores been generated by purely random behavior on the part of the pupils. (Visual perspective on differences in dispersion between a distribution of observed scores centered near a test's chance-level floor and a truly random distribution is provided in Figure 2 which contrasts the observed pretest distribution for the treatment groups and a computer-generated "completely random" counterpart).

These analyses suggest strongly that this evaluation was carried out using a test with viable properties, even in this restricted range of achievement, and that the registered NCE gain constitutes a practically useful (but possibly "attenuated") estimate of "project effects" (given the limitations of basic model assumptions for gain estimation).

The general relevance for evaluation of the particular types of analyses involved in this illustration, and their specific applicability in Title I settings, seems evident.

Responsibility for Evaluations of Chance Scores

Assessing the measurement properties of chance-level scores will require some extra effort and cost. The methods reviewed here all require additional steps in the statistical analysis, steps not ordinarily undertaken. Some of the methods require considerable sophistication. Others, while simpler, require the scoring of answer sheets. Is it reasonable to expect Title I school districts to perform such analyses for themselves? Or should there be services available to them from the scoring agencies which process the test results?

The language of the Standards for Educational and Psychological Tests (1974), jointly prepared by the American Psychological Association, the American Educational Research Association, and the National Council of

Figure 1. Cross-Tabulation of Pretest and Posttest Raw Scores MAT Elementary, Form F, Total Reading, Grade 4, Title I

Raw Score Interval Pretest	Raw Score Interval, Posttest													Total
	05–09	10–14	15–19	20–24	25–29	30–34	35–39	40–44	45–49	50–54	55–59	60–64	65–69	
65–69														( )
60–64														( )
55–59														( )
50–54													1	(1)
45–49														(–)
40–44												1		(1)
35–39						1		1	1					(6)
30–34			1	1		1		1	3					(6)
25–29				3	1	2	3	1	3					(12)
20–24				3	1	2	2	1	1					(10)
15–19	1		1	2	2	1	2	1	1		1			(11)
10–14			1				1		1					(3)
05–09														
00–04														
Total	(1)	(–)	(3)	(9)	(4)	(7)	(8)	(5)	(10)	(–)	(1)	(1)	(1)	(50)

$r = .57$

$\overline{X}_{pre} = 25.5 = PR\ 6 = NCE\ 17$

$\overline{X}_{post} = 35.0 = PR\ 10 = NCE\ 23$

$SD_{pre} = 8.3$

$SD_{post} = 12.3$

**Figure 2. Stem-Leaf Distribution of Observed and
Computer-Generated Random Scores on a
95 Item Reading Test (Four Options per Item)**

Computer Generated, Random Scores	(First Digit)	Pretest Observed Raw Scores, 4th Grade Title I Project
	9*	
	9	
N = 50	8*	N = 50
X = 24.5	8	X = 25.5
S.D. = 3.7	7*	S.D. = 8.3
	7	
	6*	
	6	
$\overline{X}_{chance}$ = 23.8	5*	
S.D.$_{chance}$ = 4.2	5	2
	4*	
	4	0
	3*	77957 8
311	3	24301 0
55 55555 66666 66788 99999	2*	79665 75568 87
001 22233 33333 44444	2	04231 23304
6 78999	1*	75785 89798 6
	1	041
	0*	
	0	

Measurement in Education is worded so as to place responsibility on the test users. Thus, Standard J5.5 states: "Ordinarily, normative interpretations of ability test scores should not be made for scores in the chance range." Standard J7 is also relevant: "The test user should consider alternative interpretations of a given score. Essential." These standards would seem to indicate that Title I districts themselves, involved in the score interpretation and as the score users, should carry out the operations which evaluate chance scores.

But the test publishers and scoring agencies bear clear professional responsibility for facilitating the proper use of tests. These agencies are as involved in the problems of reaching appropriate decisions under the guidelines as are the districts themselves. They have direct access to specially trained professional psychometric talent and, of course, computerized routines for processing and analyzing data. Moreover, certain of the statistical approaches for detecting "randomness" in a distribution of scores or in a set of individual test records are most efficiently applied at the time of initial scoring—distributional and internal consistency methods, for example—and they are applicable to data from a single testing. If a test publisher should determine that a given Title I (or other) test administration has generated a large number of "chance-level" scores, it might institute specific distributional or other tests for "randomness" and include appropriate interpretive or cautionary comments in its report to the testing district.

Distributional and internal consistency approaches to the assessment of randomness would appear to demand levels of psychometric and statistical sophistication that place them more nearly within the province of the test publisher or a scoring service than that of the local school district. On the other hand, correlational approaches involving assessment of predictive and concurrent valididty in the test scores of low-scoring Title I pupils are more clearly within the jurisdiction of the local district. The local district is in a position to develop directly the necessary matched records for cohorts of students, and correlational methods and concepts are not only more basic, but also less complicated than other methods. Moreover, they can be applied in studying questions regarding the validity of testing and to the evaluation process outside the specific context of Title I evaluation, as well as in conjunction with questions regarding the measurement utility of the tests used in the Title I evaluation. Thus, it is reasonable to infer that correlational approaches to the utility of the test score involved can and should be applied by the local district in conjunction with the implementation of norm-referenced evaluations.

Toward More Functional Guidelines for Functional-Level Testing

The fundamental purpose of the current guidelines concerning functional level testing in norm-referenced evaluation is sound. There *are* interpretive ambiguities and potential evaluation problems associated with the use in a particular setting of a test that generates a distribution of scores centered near its chance-level floor.

However, we believe that the line of reasoning developed here and the evidence that has been reviewed warrant a conclusion that the interpretive ambiguities and evaluation problems posed when a norm-referenced evaluation involves the estimation of in-level standings from the results of an "easier" out-of-level test are at least as great as those encountered in the use of a "more difficult" in-level test and, more important, considerably less amenable to resolution by local practitioners. The need for some restructuring and strengthening of the guidelines is evident. We believe that a set of guidelines formulated along the general lines outlined below might contribute to better informed decisions regarding functional level testing and better evaluation practices in local school districts.

First, reformulated guidelines should be more conservative with respect to the use of out-of-level tests. Use of more than two test levels within a single grade group should be questioned. Limitations of vertical equating should be emphasized and local evaluators should be reminded of the need for assessing the degree of comparability of scores on adjacent levels of the tests they intend to use (along the lines illustratively suggested by Stewart, 1980, for example).

Second, local evaluators should be encouraged to avoid reliance on univariate assessments based on chance-score rules of thumb as a basis for assessing basic measurement properties in observed test scores. Pretest-posttest correlation, and the correlation of test scores with other current observations of performance in relevant skill areas, should be strongly encouraged, not only in the limited sense of helping to resolve interpretive ambiguities in observed chance-range scores, but more generally as an essential procedure for interpreting evaluation results. Guidelines should emphasize the assessment of predictive and concurrent as well as content validity.

Third, test publishers can and should reinforce guidelines by providing services and conducting research designed to clarify the measurement properties of scores in the chance range, as well as by alerting test users to the hazards involved in treating scores on different tests as comparable.

References

Angoff, W. H. "Scales, Norms, and Equivalent Scores." In R. L. Thorndike (Ed.), *Educational Measurement.* Washington, D.C.: American Council on Education, 1971.

APA-AERA-NCME Standards for Educational and Psychological Tests. Washington, D.C.: American Psychological Association, 1974.

Appelbaum, W. R. "Effects of Off-Level Assignment." Paper presented at annual meeting of the American Educational Research Association, San Francisco, 1979.

Boldt, R. F. "Study of Linearity and Homoscedasticity of Test Scores in the Chance Range." *Educational and Psychological Measurement,* 1968, *28,* 47-60.

Cliff, R. "The Predictive Value of Chance-Level Scores." *Educational and Psychological Measurement,* 1958, *18,* 607-616.

Doherty, W. "Restandardization Study." In *Combined ESAA Pilot and Basic Program Evaluation: Final Study Design* (Vol. III). Santa Monica: Systems Development Corp., 1977.

Donlon, T. F., and Fischer, F. E. "An Index of an Individual's Agreement with Group-Determined Item Difficulties." *Educational and Psychological Measurement,* 1968, *28,* 105-113.

Donlon, T. F., and Rindler, S. E. "Consistency of Item Difficulty for Individuals and Groups in the Graduate Record Examination." Paper presented at annual meeting of the American Educational Research Association, San Francisco, 1979.

Echernacht, G. J. "A Note on Selection and the Norm Referenced Model" (Research Memorandum). Princeton, N.J.: Educational Testing Service, 1978.

Fowler, H. M. "An Application of the Ferguson Method of Computing Item Conformity and Person Conformity." *Journal of Experimental Education,* 1954, 237-245.

Guilford, J. P. *Psychometric Methods.* New York: McGraw-Hill, 1950.

Gulliksen, H. *Theory of Mental Tests.* New York: Wiley, 1950.

Hills, J. R., and Gladney, M. B. "Predicting Grades from Below Chance Test Scores." *Journal of Educational Measurement,* 1968, *5,* 45-53.

Hills, J. R., and Stanley, J. C. "Easier Test Improves Prediction of Black Students College Grades." *Journal of Negro Education,* 1970, *39,* 320-324.

Hopkins, K. D. "Extrinsic Reliability: Estimating and Attenuating Variance from Response Styles, Chance, and Other Irrelevant Sources." *Educational and Psychological Measurement,* 1964, *24,* 271-281.

Levine, R. D., and Lord, F. M. "An Index of the Discriminating Powers of a Test at Different Parts of the Score Range." *Educational and Psychological Measurement,* 1959, *19,* 497-500.

Levine, M. V., and Rubin, D. B. "Measuring the Appropriateness of Multiple-Choice Test Scores." *Journal of Educational Statistics,* 1979, *4,* 269-290.

Linn, R. L. "Anchor Test Study: The Long and the Short of It." *Journal of Educational Measurement,* 1975, *12,* 201-213.

Long, J. V. "Out-of-Level Survey Testing in Title I — Further Empirical Examination" (University of Rhode Island). Paper presented at annual meeting of the American Educational Research Association, San Francisco, 1979.

Long, J. V., Schaffran, J. A., and Kellogg, T. M. "Effects of Out-of-Level Survey Testing on Reading Achievement Scores of Title I, ESEA Students." *Journal of Educational Measurement,* 1977, *14,* 203–213.

Lord, F. M. "Practical Applications of Item Characteristic Curve Theory." *Journal of Educational Measurement,* 1977, *4,* 117–138.

Loret, P. G., Seder, A., Bianchini, J. C., and Vale, C. A. *Anchor Test Study: Final Report.* Princeton, N.J.: Educational Testing Service, 1972.

Loyd, B. H., and Hoover, H. D. "Vertical Equating Using the Rasch Model." *Journal of Educational Measurement,* 1980, *17,* 170, 179–193.

MacRae, P. J., and Green, D. R. "Comment by." *The Reading Teacher,* 1971, *24* (4).

Pelavin, H., and Barker, P. "The Generalizability of the Results of a Standardized Achievement Test." Paper presented at annual meeting of the American Educational Research Association, San Francisco, 1976.

Pike, L. W., and Flaugher, R. L. "Assessing the Meaningfulness of Group Responses to Multiple-Choice Test Items." Reprinted from the *Proceedings,* 78th Annual Convention, American Psychological Association, 1970.

Roberts, O. A. *Out-of-Level Testing* (ESEA Title I Evaluation and Reporting System, Technical Paper No. 6). Mountain View, Calif.: RMC Research Corp., 1976.

Roberts, S. J. *Test Floor and Ceiling Effects* (ESEA, Title 1, Evaluation & Reporting System, Technical Paper No. 15). Mountain View, Calif.: RMC Research Corp., 1978.

Slinde, J. A., and Linn, R. L. "Vertically Equated Tests: Fact or Phantom?" *Journal of Educational Measurement,* 1977, *14,* 23–32.

Slinde, J. A., and Linn, R. L. "An Exploration of the Adequacy of the Rasch Model for the Problem of Vertical Equating." *Journal of Educational Measurement,* 1978, *15,* 23–35.

Slinde, J. A., and Linn, R. L. "A Note on Vertical Equating via the Rasch Model for Groups of Quite Different Ability and Tests of Quite Different Difficulty." *Journal of Educational Measurement,* 1979, *16,* 159–165.

Stewart, B. L. "Interlevel Articulation and Title I Evaluation." Paper presented at annual meeting of the American Educational Research Association, Boston, 1980.

Tallmadge, G. K., and Wood, C. T. *User's Guide: ESEA Title I Evaluation and Reporting System.* Mountain View, Calif.: RMC Research Corp., 1978.

Wright, B. D. "Solving Measurement Problems with the Rasch Model." *Journal of Educational Measurement,* 1977, *14,* 97–116.

Kenneth M. Wilson and Thomas F. Donlon are research scientists at Educational Testing Service, Princeton, N.J.

Two of the three methods Wilson and Donlon suggest
for evaluating chance level scores are based on
an inappropriate model of examinee behavior.

Discussion:
Assessing the Reliability
and Validity of
Chance-Level Scores

Bruce L. Stewart

Wilson and Donlon suggest three strategies for assessing the reliability of chance-level scores: (1) studies of the predictive efficiency of chance-level scores for criteria such as college grades, (2) comparisons of observed score distributions with those specified by theory under the assumption of random responding, and (3) assessment of the relationship between individual response patterns and group-determined indices of item difficulty. While I agree that chance-level scores should not be assumed to be invalid or unreliable, I have reservations about the methods Wilson and Donlon propose for evaluating the measurement properties of such scores. Two of their suggested methods are based upon an inappropriate model of examinee behavior; the remaining method is not likely to meet the concerns of many local evaluators. I will devote most of my discussion to the second and third suggested methods since they seem to me to be the most practical for local Title I evaluators. Toward the end of the chapter, I will briefly indicate my difficulties with the first strategy, and offer an alternative.

Modeling Examinee Behavior

Strategies (2) and (3) are based upon a knowledge-or-random guessing model of examinee behavior. The model assumes that examinees either possess sufficient knowledge to identify the correct response among k-1 distractors, or guess randomly among the k alternatives for each item. Examinees do not generally conform to this model.

Even when an examinee does not know the correct response to an item, the responses often are not equally attractive. Sometimes one or more distractors are clearly wrong to most examinees, even though they may not know the correct answer. In such cases, examinees are likely to guess randomly among fewer than the k reponses per item. Other times, an item may contain one distractor that is particularly attractive, perhaps because it is the longest, or because it contains words that are more familiar to the examinees than those in the other responses. Despite a lack of knowledge about the correct answer, examinees do not always guess randomly among the possible alternatives.

Considerable evidence also suggests that examinees use partial information or misinformation when responding to multiple choice test items. Coombs, Milholland, and Womer (1956), for example, asked examinees to rank their degree of certainty of the incorrectness of three of four responses to items on a multiple choice test. Their data suggested that when examinees do not recognize the correct response, they still perceive some alternatives as more likely to be incorrect than others. Dressel and Schmid (1953) required examinees to mark as many of five response alternatives as needed to insure that the correct response was among those marked. They reported that over 90 percent of the test items received only one or two eliminations, suggesting that examinees did not consider each alternative equally attractive. Ebel (1968) studied students' guessing behavior and found that responses reported as blind guesses were correct slightly more often than would be expected by chance. Ebel also found the weighted average of responses students considered to be no more than blind guesses to be 5.4 percent (over four tests). Other investigators have reported similar findings.

Because examinees may often behave differently than expected under the knowledge-or-random-guessing model, the model is likely to be an inappropriate basis for examining the measurement properties of chance-level scores. When examinees can eliminate one or more responses as incorrect, their expected item score increases. The score variance for the item also increases, and will reach a maximum when examinees guess randomly between only two alternatives. If examinees can successfully eliminate incorrect alternatives for a number of items, both the mean chance score and the variance due to chance will increase. Comparisons of obtained score distributions with those generated from random responding are therefore likely to be misleading. In addition, such comparisons address only the question of whether all examinees are likely to be responding randomly. If the observed mean and variance exceed the mean chance score and the variance due to chance, respectively, this result suggests that not all examinees are responding randomly. It provides no information about the reliability or validity of those scores in the chance region, however.

Assessments of the relationship between an individual's pattern of item responses and group-determined indices of item difficulty are also likely to be affected when examinees guess randomly among fewer than the k responses per item. When examinees can eliminate incorrect alternatives, they are more likely to guess correctly on items and thereby reduce item difficulties. These items will appear to be relatively easy. The items for which examinees cannot eliminate any alternatives and are forced to respond randomly will appear more difficult. Thus, many examinees may show a pattern of correct responses on the relatively "easier" items and incorrect responses on the more difficult items — a pattern that probably would not appear suspicious. When examinees respond randomly among fewer than the k alternatives per item, comparisons of individual response patterns and group-determined indices of item difficulty are probably inappropriate.

The remaining strategy of correlating chance-level scores with other criteria to determine their predictive efficiency seems wide of the mark. A reasonable correlation between chance-level scores and standing on other criteria may be produced when some of the chance-level scores reflect random responding and others reflect genuinely low ability. A nonzero correlation does not suggest that all of the scores in the chance region are valid or reliable; it suggests only that not all of the scores are invalid or unreliable. Correlating chance-level scores with standing on other criteria represents only a partial solution to the problem of evaluating the measurement properties of chance-level scores. Such correlations provide suggestive (but weak) evidence that not all scores within the chance region are products of random responding.

An Alternative Approach

Several additional strategies are available to Title I evaluators concerned with the reliability and validity of chance-level scores. The appropriateness of the knowledge-or-random-guessing model may be tested by performing a chi-square test for independence of the responses to each item. Each distractor constitutes a cell in the table; a significant chi-square suggests that not all distractors are equally attractive. A nonsignificant result suggests that the distractors can probably be considered roughly equal in attractiveness. Results compiled over all the test items in turn will suggest whether the knowledge-or-random-guessing model is appropriate for the data.

The validity of chance-level scores may also be assessed by examining the gain-score distribution, with special attention to scores that show large changes between testings. Changes of more than twenty-five NCEs (for example), may indicate that at least one score does not represent the student's true ability. Examining the test papers of such students may provide other indications of the validity of the scores. Large numbers of omitted items or evidence of essentially random responding such as A-B-C-D, A-B-C-D, and so on, may indicate that the student's score does not fairly represent his or her ability.

Finally, the pretest-posttest correlation for scores within the chance region can be computed and compared to the same correlation for the whole group. When corrected for restriction of range, the correlation for the chance-level group should equal or closely approach the correlation for the entire group. A substantially smaller corrected correlation suggests that additional error variance is present in the chance-level scores. Presumably, this error variance is due to the increased guessing behavior of examinees who score within the chance region.

Assessing the measurement properties of chance-level scores is difficult at best. Wilson and Donlon make a valuable point that the reliability and validity of such scores should be investigated. Only a careful examination of chance-level scores can suggest whether they are likely to reflect random responding or to represent a reasonable estimate of an examinee's ability.

References

Coombs, C. H., Milholland, J. E., and Womer, F. B. "The Assessment of Partial Knowledge." *Educational and Psychological Measurement,* 1956, *16,* 13–37.

Dressel, P. L., and Schmid, J. "Some Modifications of the Multiple-Choice Item." *Educational and Psychological Measurement,* 1953, *13,* 574–595.

Ebel, R. L. "Blind Guessing on Objective Achievement Tests." *Journal of Educational Measurement,* 1968, *5,* 321–325.

Bruce L. Stewart is a research associate at RMC Research Corporation in Mountain View, California.

Wilson and Donlon's chapter views out-of-level testing
from the limited perspective of the evaluator
and not from the perspective of a student
taking the test. Motivational effects
must be considered.

Discussion:
Toward Functional Criteria
for Functional-Level Testing
in Title I Evaluation

Paul Raffeld

Wilson and Donlon outline three major recommendations regarding the use of functional-level testing. In brief, these recommendations are (1) "the Title I guidelines should be more conservative with respect to the use of out-of-level tests," (2) "local evaluators should be encouraged to avoid reliance on univariate assessments based on chance scores," and (3) "test publishers can and should reinforce guidelines."

While I agree with the intent of these recommendations and with the authors' general approach to functional-level testing, I find that their paper lacks sufficient detail with regard to their suggested alternative methods of examining test scores within the chance range. Their paper also views out-of-level testing from the limited perspective of an evaluator and not from the perspective of a student taking the test. The major thrust of my review will center on the unanswered question concerning the magnitude of a correlation that would indicate useful test data and the potential motivational effects of taking a test that is too difficult for a student to handle.

Wilson and Donlon go to considerable length to point out that test scores within the so-called chance score range do not always reflect chance responses. Nonetheless, the frequency of nonchance test scores, falling within the chance-score range, is obviously directly related to the size of the chance-score range. This range, on the other hand, is subject to a considerable degree of definitional ambiguity. A common practice noted by Wilson and Donlon is to use two standard deviations around the chance-score mean as the chance-score criterion. This range, however, is quite large and allows for a fair amount of true-score variance to be present in such test-score data. For example, in a hundred-item four-choice test, the chance score mean would be twenty-five and the upper score, using two standard deviations, would be about thirty-four. In this situation, a student could score as high as twelve points and then guess at the remaining eighty-eight items. This limited true-score variance may result in low to moderate correlations.

The real question, however, is how much relationship is needed before one can consider the test scores useful. This question is left unanswered by Wilson and Donlon. Nonetheless, it seems to be a critical element if the decision to use chance score data is to be based upon correlations, as suggested by the authors. Furthermore, it is quite possible for patterned responses to lead to spurious correlations between two testings, thus making the test-retest correlation a relatively poor index for deciding on test-score utility. Of course, if LEAs can spend the time and money to examine test scores in a variety of ways, including correlations and reliability estimates, then by all means they should do so. In most cases that I am familiar with, however, school evaluators lack the training and the time to carefully examine test data as suggested by Wilson and Donlon. Furthermore, there is no real guideline offered by the authors, as noted earlier, regarding the magnitude of the relationships necessary to decide in favor of in-level testing. It is still a matter of judgment and the quality of such decisions must depend upon experience in examining test score data.

Wilson and Donlon's argument for supporting the use of test scores within the chance-score range is based upon what they consider to be a worse alternative, out-of-level testing. Here the authors cite considerable evidence indicating that the equating of standardized tests is not adequate for the task of scoring out-of-level tests in-level. They also note that such equating problems increase when testing more than one level below (or above) the publisher's recommended level.

While this seems to be the case for many of the tests in current use, the recommendation to use on-level test-score data that reflect a relatively high proportion of chance variance is debatable. A number of the studies cited by Wilson and Donlon (Doherty Restandardization Study, 1977; Long, Schaffran, and Kellogg, 1977; Pelavin and Barker, 1976) reflect some consistency in the way out-of-level test scores over- or underestimate on-level scores. To the extent that such consistency exists, gains might be estimated within some specifiable margin of error. It may also be possible to derive some adjustment factor for those tests that behave in a fairly consistent manner.

What is needed are studies that focus on the difference in gain estimates obtained from in-level and out-of-level test administration to low-scoring students. In this way, we may be able to estimate the degree to which either or both methods lead to biased estimates of gain. Wilson and Donlon recommend that the test publishers become involved at this level and I fully agree. Until such studies are conducted, however, it will be difficult to support one method as being better than the other.

There is no doubt that the very logic of out-of-level testing is strained, as noted by the authors, when attempting to use levels that differ widely in content. For this reason alone, caution concerning how far out-of-level one should go is needed. When students are doing so poorly that they require a test level several levels below that recommended by the publisher, the test will have utility only for the classroom teacher and not for evaluation purposes. Nevertheless, if a teacher wants to know what content area a student can handle, the administration of out-of-level tests may be the best method of getting the answer.

Even if test scores within the chance-score range can be shown to correlate in a valid way with other variables, there is some question as to the use of in-level testing. For the most part, standardized tests are designed to measure the maximum performance, not typical performance. Therefore, the assumption that students are highly motivated to take a test is generally made. To the extent that such motivation is attenuated, test-score validity becomes questionable. The evidence of such motivation is found when a student attempts all items; giving careful consideration to each question and the alternatives. However, students who meet with repeated failure at the beginning of a test are not likely to continue to interact with each item as the test publisher had intended.

Unfortunately, the process of testing in-level for low-scoring students becomes self-defeating, since the student is consistently punished or at least fails to receive any reward for the effort of taking the test. Such a cycle, once started, is difficult to break unless the student is given the opportunity to experience some degree of success. Therefore, unless there is some clearcut evidence that in-level test scores are significantly more consistent and less biased than in-level test scores derived from one level below, it would seem to be better to recommend testing out-of-level for those students scoring at or below the chance score mean.

For the purposes of program evaluation, we need test scores that are sufficiently reliable and valid to produce an accurate picture of program impact. However, in our present state of technology regarding standardized testing, I seriously doubt if the issue of magnitude of program impact can be addressed with any precision. At best, we can probably say that a program had some positive effect or failed to demonstrate such effects. At this level of sophistication, it seems a bit of a waste to concentrate on small differences in the magnitude of gain estimates unless it can be shown that such differences indeed reflect significant program impact. The question of educational significance, however, has yet to be resolved. Under these conditions, why not make the test taking chore a little easier on those students for whom the test is far too difficult. This would be especially true if the risk of bias in gain scores were minimal when compared to using in-level scores in the chance-score range.

58

References

Doherty, W. "Restandardization Study." In *Combined ESAA Pilot and Basic Program Evaluations: Final Study Design.* (Vol. 3.) Santa Monica: Systems Development Corp., 1977.

Long, J. V., Schaffran, J. A., and Kellogg, T. M. "Effects of Out-of-Level Survey Testing on Reading Achievement Scores of Title I ESEA Students." *Journal of Educational Measurement,* 1977, *14,* 203–213.

Pelavin, H., and Barker, P. "The Generalizability of the Results of a Standardized Achievement Test." Paper presented at annual meeting of the American Educational Research Association, San Francisco, 1976.

*Paul Raffeld is director of the Region VI ESEA Title I
Technical Assistance Center for Powell Associates
in Austin, Texas.*

*"Regression toward the mean" remains a source of argument,
confusion, and error, despite seventy years of explanations,
lay to didactic, kindly and otherwise. Some historical
background, simulations, pictures, and even simple
math may help. Regression after use of a fallible
test for selection is a special case.*

Regression Toward the Mean and the Regression-Effect Bias

A. O. H. Roberts

Work Involves Friction and Produces Heat and Light

Perhaps every applied statistician worth his salt has said to himself at some time, "I understand regression-towards-the-mean; others only think they do." The correlation coefficient alone, one parent of the regression coefficient (variance ratio is the other), is subject to more persistent misunderstanding and misuse than is the offspring. The abrupt change in direction from an earlier statistical mainline prompted by Galton's genius has been poorly recognized, surely contributing to the volume of misuse of both correlation and regression.

Particularly in the higher echelons, the topic seems to spark strong feelings. Edgeworth tried to generalize the concept of regression for the multivariate case and, perhaps deservedly, came under Karl Pearson's lash, "I think he harnessed imperfect mathematical analysis to a jolting car and drove it into an Irish bog on his road" (Pearson, 1920, p. 29). Recently, Campbell and Erlebacher (1970, p. 185) wrote of a regression procedure that it led to "tragically misleading misanalyses." After dealing with a dozen articles published over a

Preparation of this chapter was supported in part by a contract from the U.S. Office of Education/Office of Evaluation and Dissemination. However, the opinions expressed here do not necessarily reflect their position or policy and no official endorsement by the Office of Education should be inferred.

period of thirty years, they conclude that 99 percent of experts would mistakenly recommend analysis of covariance as a correction. Overall and Woodward (1977a and 1977b) provide some defense for that procedure. Kenny (1975, p. 345, 348, and 356) agrees with Campbell and Erlebacher, and believes that in many cases gain scores, in the form of standardization change-score analysis, are preferable. But Cronbach and Furby (1970, p. 68) argue that "gain scores are rarely useful no matter how they may be adjusted or refined."

With Campbell and Erlebacher (1970) one should read Cook and Campbell (1976, p. 277) who say of examinees classified on the basis of unreliable tests, that there is a threat of crediting differential change to the treatment, when statistical regression is the cause. Yet when the Title I Evaluation and Reporting System set out to avoid this trap by insisting on separation of selection test and pretest, Glass (1978) said of the authors that their "misconception was firmly entrenched . . . to let them (examinees) get all the regressing out of their system."

Some think that the very term "regression" leads to misunderstanding and blame Galton: "Apparently Galton did not initially recognize the ubiquity of this phenomenon" (Hopkins and Glass, 1978, p. 154); "Regression toward the mean is not some immutable law of nature. . . . The interpretation of such results as a 'regression toward mediocrity' has been aptly called the regression fallacy" (Hays and Winkler, 1971, p. 628); "Regression is a statistical phenomenon. Biological regression in only one possible interpretation" (Humphreys, 1978, p. 1317); "The term 'regression' is not a particularly happy one from an etymological point of view" (Yule and Kendall, 1950, p. 213).

Historical Background for Regression Theory

Between the years 1869 and 1906, Galton wrote some thirty-one articles and two books on a topic of the most enduring interest to him — heredity — partly as a result of the impact of his cousin Darwin's work. Galton experimented with sweetpeas, moths, rabbits and dogs, later including his best-known observations on human data and pedigrees. His investigations covered blood transfusions in rabbits, colors of horses, sizes of sweetpeas, temper in families, transmission of genius, and stature of sons and daughters as related to the mid-parent height — and it was this study that yielded the terms "reversion," (from which came the symbol r) "regression towards mediocrity," and "the law of filial regression." His *Memories of My Life* (1908) throws light both on his choice of terms, and on one of the sources of perpetual confusion to his successors. He asks (1908, p. 300):

> How is it possible for a population to remain alike in its features during many successive generations if the *average* produce of each couple resemble their parents? Their children are not alike but vary: therefore, some would be taller, some shorter than their average height; so among the issue of a gigantic couple there would usually be some children more gigantic still. Conversely, as to very small couples . . .

He then does a carefully controlled experiment (with the help of many friends) on the sizes of two generations of sweetpea seeds: "The result clearly proved *Regression;* the mean filial deviation was only one-third that of the parental one" (1908, p. 301).

Galton has recognized that the species sets limits (like the cushions of a billiard table) within which heredity must operate; and that the nearer to one or other cushion, the greater the likelihood or freedom of movement in the opposite direction. Without this limitation, the variance of height would increase indefinitely with the generations.

Galton had met Quetelet (pioneer in the application of the Gaussian curve to demography); in turn, Quetelet had spent some time with each of Laplace and Gauss. Galton describes the previous applications of "the law, commonly known to mathematicians as that of 'frequency of error'" and then: "Its application had been extended by Quetelet to the proportions of the human body, on the grounds that the differences, say in stature, between men of the same race might *theoretically* be treated as if they were errors made by nature in her attempt to mould individual man of the same race according to the same ideal pattern" (Galton, 1972, p. 28). From a later source there is this pregnant statement: "The primary objects of the Gaussian Law of Error were exactly opposed, in one sense, to those to which I applied them. They were to get rid of, or to provide a just allowance for errors. But these errors or deviations were the very things I wanted to preserve and to know about" (1908, p. 301).

There is the point. The Gaussian development was based upon an assumption of accurate measurement (as of true angular descriptions of star positions) submerged in irrelevant and random error. Galton on the other hand, wanted to disentangle two real and accurate, but confounded, sources of measurement. He wanted, not to discover "true" height, as opposed to "observed," but to allocate the proportionate contributions of heredity, and of the inherent restrictions of the species, in the determination of height. He was honing a tool fo a special task, one closer to the later work of Spearman (his two-factor theory) than to the equations of Kuder and Richardson. In this he is following Quetelet.

Where Laplace and Gauss had concerned themselves with truth and error, Galton looked at the geometry of his data and perceived the operation of two independent truths. In the end "the law of frequency and error" becomes a special case of his more general apprehension of two or more independent forces at work; and he is simply not interested in that special case. "Regression to mediocrity" is the manifestation of an independent but important operator at work. Galton's key is this: An individual's deviation from the population median (or mean) height is the sum of his deviations from his median genetic factor, and from his median environmental factor. Using common symbols, we would write:

$$(H_i - \mu_h) = (G_i - \mu_g) + (E_i - \mu_e)$$

and if we observe many such individuals, we could "standardize" from their collective deviations and get, following Burt (1971),

$$S_h^2 = S_g^2 + S_e^2 + 2S_gS_e r_{ge} \tag{1}$$

in which "e" stands for "environment," not "error." But it could as well have been "error," for this is a general linear equation for composite variances. Such a mathematical statement certainly demonstrates the global insight of the theoretical statistician, and is useful for the production of more specialized equations. The t-test for uncorrelated means, the phi-coefficient, the rank-order correlation and the split-half reliability correction are all examples of special-purpose condensations from more general statements of composite variances and covariances. Yet that penchant of the theoretician for the elimination of distinctions, helpful as it is for him, can be a handicap for the practitioner, for whom the clear recognition of a special goal is as important as the specialized vehicle he uses to attain it; Quetelet and Galton were such practitioners. So were Spearman and Brown, or Kuder and Richardson. We both honor the workman and recognize the goal when we attach his name or an abbreviation of it to a routine calculation such as Spearman-Rank Order, Kuder-Richardson Reliability, T-score, F-test, and so on. In fact, it would seem that the only reason that Pearson (1920) had for denying recognition to Bravais as the inventor of correlation (who as early as 1846 had given one form of the equation, xy/NS_xS_y), and giving it rather to Galton (who had instead perceived the significance of regression) was that Galton had a clearer goal. Now we credit Pearson with the invention!

We often coin terms to denote special cases of more general concepts. For example, a standard error is only a special case of a standard deviation, a reliability coefficient is only a special case of correlation. Let us be consistent and recognize the Regression Effect Bias as a special case of "regression towards the mean"—which it is; for example, see English and English (1958, p. 450). Our recognition restores Gauss's "error" to the central position from which Galton had evicted it, while retaining Galton's extension of the reasoning to the bivariate case.

Composites of Truth and Errors

Where X_i is an observed value, T_i the true value, and E_i an error, Gauss would have written $X_i = T_i + E_i$, and then,

$$S_X^2 = S_T^2 - S_E^2 \tag{2}$$

After Galton and Pearson we would write more generally, where G_i and S_i are two part-scores of X_i

$$X_i = G_i + S_i$$

and then $\qquad S_X^2 = S_g^2 + S_s^2 + 2S_gS_s r_{gs} \tag{3}$

And if $\qquad Y_i = G_i + T_i$

$$S_y^2 = S_g^2 + S_t^2 + 2S_gS_t r_{gt} \tag{4}$$

More important, using composite covariance and variances, we would find that

$$r_{xy} = \frac{S_g^2 + S_g S_s r_{gs} + S_g S_t r_{gt} + S_s S_t r_{st}}{\sqrt{(S_g^2 + S_s^2 + 2S_g S_s r_{gs})\,(S_g^2 + S_t^2 + 2S_g S_t r_{gt})}} \tag{5}$$

If now for any reason we have chosen variates X and Y in which there is no relationship at all between part-scores G, S and T (the measures are orthogonal), equation (5) would simplify to

$$r_{xy} = \frac{S_g^2}{\sqrt{(S_g^2 + S_s^2)\,(S_g^2 + S_t^2)}} \tag{6}$$

For example, if X_i were parental-mid-height, Y_i filial height, G_i the hereditary or genetic part of height, and S_i and T_i specific or environmental contributions to parental and filial heights respectively, the correlation would have a ceiling of unity only if both S_s^2 and S_t^2 were zero. Furthermore, if $S_x^2 = S_y^2$, which it was in Galton's example, the correlation coefficient and the regression coefficient would have been the same. In fact, we could write

$$r_{xy} = \frac{S_g^2}{S_x^2} \tag{7}$$

and in Galton's original reasoning, this would represent the proportion of all variance in height that was due only to heredity. The proportion of variance attributable to the specific contribution is

$$1 - r_{xy} = \frac{S_g^2}{S_x^2} \tag{8}$$

Returning now to the problem of true and observed measures, using Gauss's approach in addition to Galton's, we would still find that there is no direct way of deriving a true measurement from an observed one. However, finding two or more different results *when no difference should be expected* would reflect the existence of error; and the variance of many such differences would be a measure of the variance of error. To be more precise, it would be twice the variance of the difference, or error between the observed, and the unknown true values, since the "best" estimate for each of the latter would be the average of the two observed measures. If discrepancies between repeated measurements are evidence of the involvement of error, then the correlation coefficient between the two sets is an immediate index of the dependability of reliability of the measure. Can it be used to estimate the size of the error variance?

In equation (5) above we need only rename the two specifics S_i and T_i, error-at-first-measurement and error-at-second-measurement and the equation becomes relevant to our problem though not yet useful. We can replace the two parenthetical terms in the denominator by their original observed equivalents S_x^2 and S_y^2, but that would still leave us with too many undeterminable quantities in the numerator, even though the correlation itself could be calculated. We therefore make an *operational* simplification. We will imagine there to be substitutes for X_i, Y_i, S_i, and T_i, namely X_i', Y_i', and T_i', such that

$$X_i' = G_i + S_i'$$

$$Y_i' = G_i + T_i', \text{ but so that}$$

$$r_{gs'} = r_{gt'} + r_{s't'} = 0$$

and now equation (5) takes the form of (6).

Notice that we are not claiming that no correlation exists between the original elements; we are using substitutes that have this property. Nor is it necessary to conceive of each individual as possessing and operating his own random number generator to produce a supplement to his true score; we just find it convenient and mathematically appropriate to treat part of his obtained score or other behavior *as if* it were the product of a pseudorandom number generator.

If from equations (5) and (6) we make $S_x^2 = S_y^2$ as before, (we are measuring the same sample, using the same measuring instrument) and using the subscript e for error, instead of the specifics S and T, we have from equation (8) above

$$\frac{S_e^2}{S_x^2} = 1 - r_{xy}$$

or, in its more familiar form

$$S_e = S_x\sqrt{1 - r_{xy}} \tag{9}$$

Thus, we see that we can have the regression towards the mean envisaged by Galton, in which G, S, and T are all important secondary measures; and we can have regression in the very situation that Galton steered away from, namely where S and T were evanescent but obscuring error. We can even have a double source of regression, if we have the situation

$$X_i = G_i + S_i + e_1$$

$$Y_i = G_i + T_i + e_2.$$

This is perhaps the one postulated by Glass in which the attempt to allow for e_1 by repeating the measure X, gets only part of the regression "out of their system," when this second measure Y is later related to X. We will take this up later.

Reliability Coefficients are Created Unequal

There is another problem, explicitly recognized, among others, by Boruch and Creager (1972). There are several easily recognizable contributing sources of error, but although we refer to the "reliability of the test," the full statement should add "seen through the eyes of this group on this occasion" with additional provisoes for the purists. We can then write linear equations with a separate e_j for each identifiable source. In looking at these we do not need to worry too much about conditions that apply more or less uniformly to the whole group, while leaving their rank orders little changed. More important are sources that act *differentially* on the individuals in the group. For example, individuals have their own cyclic and erratic ups and downs like mornings-after-the-night-before. These make it necessary to take the *occasion* into account in adding e's, or in planning replications, since the occasion more than anything else will add "correlated error." Suppose that we have

$$X_i = G_i + e_1 + e_2$$

$$Y_i = G_i + e_3 + e_4$$

we can use equation (5) again as the basis or model.

We can make some or all of the r's in the numerator of the correlation coefficient disappear operationally; but if we want to compare results from different types of replications, or to use the result for "correction for attenuation," we must use some care. One case in particular needs special attention. If e_1 and e_3 are the products of a single occasion, we ought not to regard them in the same way as e_2 and e_4. Instead we should write

$$r_{xy} = \frac{S_g^2 + S_{e_1}S_{e_3}r_{e_1e_3}}{S_xS_y} \tag{10}$$

For the same test and group but for two separate occasions the correlation $r_{e_1e_3}$ will become zero. Now of course the question arises, how does one define "occasion?" We will take this up again later. In the meanwhile any reliability of the so-called Internal Consistency type, including Split-Half with the Spearman-Brown correction, the Kuder-Richardson Formula 20 and coefficient alpha can be regarded as a single-occasion figure, while the Test-Retest, or Alternate Form methods, usually separated by a couple of weeks, are two-occasion figures. Since the uses to which a test is to be put are very rarely for prediction or estimation within the day, single-occasion reliabilities are seldom appropriate.

Additional Theory of the Regression-Effect Bias

Let us suppose that for a single group we have two applications of the same test, or of alternate forms, with about two weeks between and no real change in underlying levels of the attribute in individuals being tested. The results of both adminstrations are standardized to the same mean and standard deviation. Figure 1 below applies.

Next, we impose a sharp cut-off or selection score on the first test, dividing the total group into two mutually exclusive subgroups, for each of which means, standard deviations, correlations, and other statistics can be computed for the univariate and bivariate distributions. This mutual exclusiveness will have some important consequences. In Figure 1 linear regression is assumed.

As long as the cut-off score X_c is above the minimum and below the maximum score, the following will hold true (where the select group is below the cut-off):

1. The mean of the select group, $\bar{X}_s$ will always be below both X_c and the total group mean $\bar{X}_t$. That for the reject group, $\bar{X}_r$ will always be above both X_c and $\bar{X}_t$.
2. $\bar{Y}_r$ exceeds $\bar{Y}_t$ which in turn exceeds $\bar{Y}_s$
3. Differences between means on X exceed corresponding differences on Y.
4. The total group SD exceeds both subgroups' SDs.
5. For each of the select and the reject groups, the variance of error for text X will be smaller than it is for the total group.
6. For each subgroup, however, the variance of error for test Y will be unaffected, and will be the same as that for the total group, *provided that variances of all Y arrays were initially equal.*

Figure 1. Effects of Selection

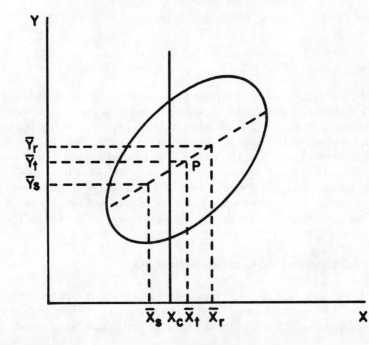

Each of the above points is either self-evident, or the proof is easily found. Point (5) depends on the fact that if the range of a composite score is restricted, the range of each subscore is restricted. Point (6) does demand homoscedasticity; but since there is no restriction of range on the test Y, variances are not restricted. However, there is a seventh point, which is less obvious though very important:

7. *Whatever the initial total group correlation between true score and error* (that is, even if it was nonzero), *there will be a negative trend to that relationship in each of the subgroups.* Thus, if initially there was a zero correlation between true score and error, in both subgroups there will now be negative correlations; and in most practical situations this will be appreciable, with very important results.

Not only is this outcome somewhat hidden, but I have so far found only one reference to it: Levin (1975, p. 117) says "It can also be shown that true score and error become negatively correlated." It occurs even if the original bivariate distribution of true scores and error is nonnormal.

Where $X_i = T_i + E_i$, we have seen from equations (7) and (8) that we can write

$$\frac{S_t}{S_x} = \sqrt{r_{xx}} \text{ and } \frac{S_e}{S_x} = \sqrt{1 - r_{xx}},$$

where r_{xx} is a two-occasion reliability. (Note that by convention, the radicals are taken as positive.)

We can standardize scores:

$$Z_x = \frac{X - \bar{X}}{S_x}$$

$$= \frac{(T + E) - (\bar{T} + \bar{E})}{S_x}$$

$$= \frac{(T - \bar{T}) + (E - \bar{E})}{S_x}$$

$$= \frac{T - \bar{T}}{S_t} \cdot \frac{S_t}{S_x} + \frac{E - \bar{E}}{S_e} \cdot \frac{S_e}{S_x}$$

$$= Z_t \sqrt{r_{xx}} + Z_e \sqrt{1 - r_{xx}}$$

So now, where $Z_{x(c)}$ is the standardized equivalent to the constant cutoff on the observed test score, we will have corresponding standardized cut-off values $Z_{t(c)}$ and $Z_{e(c)}$ related by the linear equation

$$Z_{e(c)} = \frac{Z_{x(c)}}{\sqrt{1 - r_{xx}}} - \frac{Z_{t(c)} \sqrt{r_{xx}}}{\sqrt{1 - r_{xx}}} \tag{11}$$

In this equation, $\dfrac{Z_{x(c)}}{\sqrt{1-r_{xx}}}$ is the intercept; the coefficient $-\sqrt{\dfrac{r_{xx}}{1-r_{xx}}}$ is the slope of the line; note that it is negative. With standardized scores, and with this line sketched in, even a non-normal bivariate distribution would appear as in Figure 2.

The negative relationship between true scores and error in both subgroups seems obvious. The mathematical equation demonstrates this more clearly. Its derivation is a bit tedious and will not be given here.

Where $\dfrac{s_x}{\sigma_x}$ is the ratio of the standard deviation for the selected group to that of the total group, ϱ_{xx} the reliability for the total group and $r_{te'}$ the resultant correlation of true score and error in the selected group:

$$r_{te'} = \frac{\dfrac{S_x^2}{\sigma_x^2} - 1}{\sqrt{\left(\dfrac{S_x^2}{\sigma_x^2} - 1\right)^2 + \dfrac{S_x^2}{\sigma_x^2}} = \dfrac{1}{\varrho_{xx}(1 - \varrho_{xx})}}$$

Since $\dfrac{S_x^2}{\sigma_x^2} < 1$, the numerator is negative; the denominator is positive by convention, and so the correlation $r_{te'}$ must be negative.

A more general equation can be written for the case where even $r_{te'}$ (that is, the correlation for the total-group true score and error) is not zero.

Figure 2. Negative Slope of Selection Line in True–Error Distribution

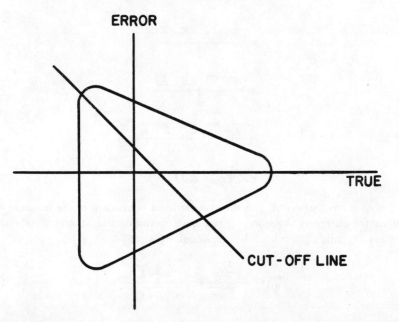

However, further simplification is more profitable. In the special case where the distribution of true and error scores is bivariate normal for the whole group, we can get an idea of the size of the $r_{te'}$'s for various reliabilities and cut-off scores (see Table 1).

A typical value for $r_{te'}$ for a Title I group would be for a cut-off at -0.25 standard deviations, with a whole group reliability of 0.80, which would yield a correlation between true and error scores of -0.441. Significant as this value is, it markedly understates the true position; it assumes a linear regression of error on true score, whereas the true regression line is almost a hyperbola, as can be seen in Figure 3.

The cut-off line is determined by equation (11) above. If we assume a bivariate normal distribution with a zero correlation between true score and error for the total group, then all relevant parameters including the resultant correlation between true and error scores can be determined for the select group. The equation for the true regression line is complex, though it is easy to plot using tables for, and mathematical properties of, the normal distribution.

Since these equations and diagrams deal with quantities as unobservable as protons and electrons, they may seem academic. However, they do serve to illustrate some important practical consequences of using uncorrected values from a single test application for both selection *and* for pretest measurement.

1. In the select group, true score and error have become negatively correlated, so that positive error supplements low true score to reject individuals wrongly, and negative error supplements some true scores to bring them wrongly into the select group.

2. The true regression curve can be divided roughly into three sections—perhaps more than coincidentally, the linear regression line does this quite efficiently: (a) From a true score of about -1.5 sigma downwards, where the correlation is virtually zero, and the curve almost perfectly linear (misclassification will be rare in this region); (b) From a true score of about -0.3

Table 1. Correlation Between True Score and Error in the Selected Group as a Function of Test Reliability for Total Group and the Cutoff Score

Cutoff Score Z_x						
Lower Limit of Upper Group or	Upper Limit of Lower Group			r_{xx} or $(1 - r_{xx})$		
		.50	.60	.70	.80	.90	.99
$-.75$	$+.75$	$-.285$	$-.280$	$-.263$	$-.231$	$-.176$	$-.059$
$-.50$	$+.50$	$-.346$	$-.340$	$-.320$	$-.283$	$-.216$	$-.073$
$-.25$	$+.25$	$-.407$	$-.400$	$-.378$	$-.336$	$-.258$	$-.088$
$.00$	$.00$	$-.467$	$-.460$	$-.436$	$-.389$	$-.302$	$-.105$
$+.25$	$-.25$	$-.524$	$-.516$	$-.491$	$-.441$	$-.346$	$-.121$
$+.50$	$-.50$	$-.577$	$-.569$	$-.543$	$-.492$	$-.390$	$-.139$
$+.75$	$-.75$	$-.625$	$-.617$	$-.591$	$-.539$	$-.433$	$-.157$

Figure 3. An Example of True and Linear Regression of Error on True Scores After Selection

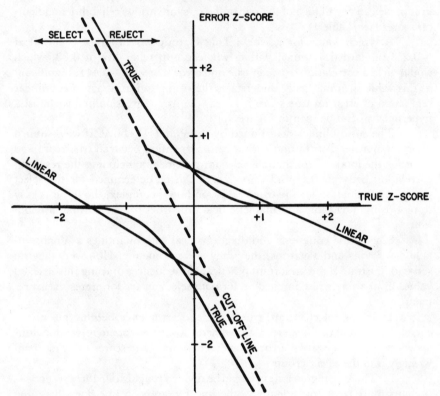

upwards, in which the regression is again almost linear, but with a very high negative correlation (equivalent to about −0.8) between true and error contributions—this part is, not surprisingly, very close to the cut-off line (a substantial proportion of misclassifications will be found here); and (c) A relatively short transitional curve links the two initially straight lines (a small proportion of misclassifications will be found over this range). A similar true regression curve is shown for the reject group, with the cut-off line above the X-axis and the positive branch of the X-axis as asymptotes. *These two true regression curves show that the individuals with a high risk of being misclassified are those within a fairly narrow band on either side of the cut-off line.*

3. The negative slope of the cut-off line is a function of the reliability only. It can swing from horizontal (for $r_{tt} = 0$) to vertical (for $r_{tt} = 1$). The lower the reliability, the higher will the negative correlation be between true score and error. The more stringent the cut-off (that is, the smaller the proportion selected) the higher will the negative correlation be between true score and error.

Understanding the generation of this negative correlation is very important. The cut-off score is a barrier which on one side traps some individuals whose unusually low errors were an insufficient supplement to adequate true scores, to push their observed scores to the right side of the line. On the other side of the barrier we have caught some individuals who had relatively low true scores but unusually high errors, so that the observed sum of the two put them also on the wrong side of the barrier. Each group then contains an excess of individuals (more particularly from those who were closest to the cut-off) with a temporary negative correlation between their true ability and error. This results in a mean score which is biased down on the left of the cut-off and up on the right.

On retesting each of these two groups with a test which has no other basis than true score for correlation with the first, however, the absence of any new barriers allows the independence of true score and error score to reassert itself. The resulting means will represent the unbiased estimates of the mean ability of each group. This fact has considerable significance: *Selection based on observed test score is a source of bias; and all bias from this source disappears at the first new test for which there is no new constraint from selection.* Note that we have not abolished random error; we have merely banished the bias that resulted from selected errors.

This negative correlation will also occur on either side of the barrier in Galton's case of two real factors; but it will not disappear upon retesting. There is also a whole class of problems that will not be touched on in this chapter: It is impossible to have conditions under which the temporary stresses to the relationship between two part scores have more limited creation in the first test, or only a partial release in the second.

We can test our perceptions by means of simulated true scores and error scores, which are then combined to yield "observed" test scores for each of two test applications. First we prepare three columns of random numbers with these properties:

1. In each column, the frequencies are roughly normal. (This is not essential, but it adds verisimilitude.)
2. Intercorrelations between columns must be at or near zero.
3. The variances of the last two columns should be roughly equal, and the variance of the first should be such as to match the predetermined "reliability" of the test, since

$$r_{tt} = \frac{S_t^2}{S_t^2 + S_e^2}$$

so

$$S_t^2 = \frac{S_e^2 r}{1 - r}$$

(If initially we make the variances of the three columns equal, we simply multiply each number in the first column by $\sqrt{r/1 - r}$.)

We now generate "Selection Test" and "Pretest" scores for each "pupil" by adding pairs of numbers from column 1 and column 2, and again column 1 and column 3. This has been done in Table 2.

Table 2. Simulation of Regression-Effect Error

Student Number	(True + Error 1)	Selection Test	Selected	(True + Error 2)	Pretest
1	(1 + 5)	6	0	(1 + 6)	7
2	(2 + 2)	4	0	(2 + 4)	6
3	(2 + 7)	9	0	(2 + 3)	5
4	(3 + 4)	7	0	(3 + 4)	7
5	(3 + 4)	7	0	(3 + 6)	9
6	(3 + 5)	8	0	(3 + 6)	9
7	(4 + 3)	7	0	(4 + 4)	8
8	(4 + 7)	11		(4 + 6)	10
9	(4 + 9)	13		(4 + 2)	6
10	(4 + 7)	11		(4 + 5)	9
11	(5 + 2)	7	0	(5 + 5)	10
12	(5 + 6)	11		(5 + 5)	10
13	(5 + 1)	6	0	(5 + 9)	14
14	(5 + 6)	11		(5 + 8)	13
15	(5 + 6)	11		(5 + 7)	12
16	(6 + 5)	11		(6 + 4)	10
17	(6 + 5)	11		(6 + 5)	11
18	(6 + 8)	14		(6 + 7)	13
19	(6 + 3)	9	0	(6 + 3)	9
20	(7 + 6)	13		(7 + 3)	10
21	(7 + 5)	12		(7 + 5)	12
22	(7 + 4)	11		(7 + 2)	9
23	(8 + 4)	12		(8 + 1)	9
24	(8 + 8)	16		(8 + 8)	16
25	(9 + 3)	12		(9 + 7)	16

Total Group					
Mean	(5 + 5)	10		(5 + 5)	10
s.d.	2 and 2	2.8282		2 and 2	2.8282
Correlation	$r_{tel} = 0.00$		$r_{xy} = 0.50$ $r_{e1e2} = 0.00$	$r_{te2} = 0.00$	

Select group					
Mean		7.0			8.4
Correlation	$r_{tel} = -0.61$			$r_{te2} = 0.08$	

On the basis of the selection test, the ten lowest-scoring students (with scores of 9 and below) were selected; notice that if we had been able to select on the true scores, students 8, 9, and 10 would have been chosen instead of students 11, 13, and 19. Five of the six named had true scores of 4 or 5, and only one had a 6; their *observed* scores ranged from 6 through 11. Had we been able to classify perfectly, the cut-off would have been a true score of 4½; only one of out actual misclassifications was more than one-quarter of a true-score standard deviation on the wrong side of the line, and that with a reliability of only 0.50!

As expected, the correlation of true score with error for the ten selected students has become negative (– 0.61); again as expected, the corresponding correlation at the pretest is back, virtually, to zero (0.08). However, of more practical importance, the mean of their selection test scores was 7.0, but of their pretest scores was 8.4 — an apparent gain of 1.4, or about one-half standard deviation. This is the result of "regression toward the mean," (though it is a special case of it). In other words, if we had used the selection test scores as the starting position, *without* the benefit of a separate pretest, then at the posttest we would have found a spurious gain of about half a standard deviation. Can we not "correct" the mean of these students' selection test scores to estimate the pretest mean, thus saving the trouble of retesting?

We have always been able to predict a dependent variate from an independent, given the necessary statistics including the correlation coefficient:

$$Y' = \varrho_{xy}\frac{\sigma_y}{\sigma_x}(X - \mu_x) + \mu_y$$

In our case this simplifies, since we are ostensibly dealing with a parallel test, so that $\sigma_y = \sigma_x$, $\mu_x = \mu_y$, and ϱ_{xy} is the reliability of the test; so, where X_s is the mean test score of the select group, X_g that for the total group, r_{gg} the reliability for the total group, and X_{cs} the corrected mean for the select group

$$X_{cs} = r_{gg}(X_s - X_g) + X_g \tag{12}$$

Notice that in our case X_s will be smaller than X_g, so that the difference in the parentheses will be negative. What is happening can be seen graphically in Figure 4.

If we actually applied the alternate form of the test to the select group, they would get a mean score, not of X_s, but of X_{cs}, a higher value. This value on the ordinate lies on the intersection of the vertical from X_s on the abscissa, and the regression line, and can be determined by subtracting from the group mean X_g, the amount AB; or we can write

$$X_{cs} = X_s + (CD)$$

$$= X_s + (BE)$$

$$= X_s + (AE - AB)$$

$$= X_s + (DE - AB)$$

$$= X_s + (X_g - X_s) - r_{gg}(X_g - X_s)$$

$$= X_s + (X_g - X_s)(1 - r_{gg})$$

Adjustments to Reliability Coefficients

However, there are still some problems to be solved before equation (12) can be made useful. In the first place, the reliability coefficient r_{gg} is that which

Figure 4. Relation of Corrected Mean to Obtained Mean
After Selection

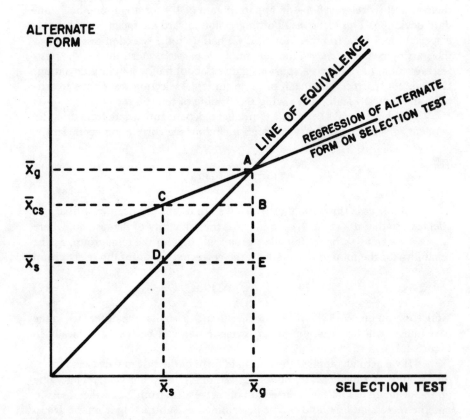

ALTERNATE
FORM

LINE OF EQUIVALENCE

REGRESSION OF ALTERNATE
FORM ON SELECTION TEST

$\overline{X}_g$

$\overline{X}_{cs}$

$\overline{X}_s$

A

C   B

D   E

$\overline{X}_s$ $\overline{X}_g$ SELECTION TEST

applies to the total group tested for selection purposes; the figures quoted in the test publisher's manuals apply to the population, of which our group is almost certain to be a nonrandom sample. If the test variance in our group is different from that in the population (usually smaller), the reliability coefficient will either have to be independently determined, or the publisher's figure will have to be adjusted first. Independent determination would necessitate a second application of the test; if we did that, we might as well do so to the select group alone, using this mean as an empirically correct value.

Fortunately, a formula for the necessary adjustment to the population reliability coefficient already exists; where r_{gg} is the figure we need, ϱ_{xx} that for the population, and s and σ are the standard deviations of test scores in our total group and the population respectively. (See, for example, Peters and Van Voorhis, 1940, p. 209; Guilford, 1956, p. 458.) This is a simple derivation from equation (8):

$$r_{gg} = 1 - \frac{\sigma^2}{s^2}(1 - \varrho_{xx}) \tag{13}$$

We can substitute (13) in equation (12) above, so that

$$\bar{X}_{cs} = 1 - \frac{\sigma^2}{s^2}(1 - \varrho_{xx})(\bar{X}_s - \bar{X}_g) + \bar{X}_g$$

$$= \bar{X}_s + \frac{\sigma^2}{s^2}(1 - \varrho_{xx})(\bar{X}_g - \bar{X}_s) \qquad (14)$$

There is one last hurdle to cross. Some publishers quote both single-occasion reliabilities (for example, Kuder–Richardson 20, coefficient alpha, or corrected split-half), and two-occasion reliabilities (for example, Alternate Form or Test-Retest); some give only one or the other. Since our ultimate comparison involves two fairly widely separated test applications (pretest or selection test, and posttest), we need to know the reliability uninflated by uncontrolled circumstances of the single occasion; that is, we need two-occasion reliabilities. Use of a KR 20, for example, would undercorrect and thus spuriously inflate gains. We therefore need some way of estimating a two-occasion reliability when only KR 20 or split-half reliabilities are available. A tabulation of all reliabilities given by seven of the well-known test publishers has been prepared by S. J. Roberts. Rough analyses of these results show that, where two reliabilities are given for one form of a test,

1. Alternate Form ≈ Test-retest – 0.01.
2. KR 20 ≈ Corrected split-half – 0.006.
3. "Few days" Alternate Form ≈ KR 20 – 0.03.
4. "Two- to three-weeks" Alternate Form ≈ KR20 – 0.09.

Since in practice the range of KR 20 values is small, it seems reasonable to use this last estimate in equation (14) whenever the KR 20 value only is known; an error in this correction of $\pm$ e will lead to an error in the estimate of X_{cs}.

$$\text{Error of estimate} = -\frac{\sigma^2}{s^2} \cdot e(\bar{X}_g - \bar{X}_s)$$

or expressing this as a proportion of the correction to X_s, where C_t is the true correction and C_0 the obtained,

$$C_t - C_o = \pm C_t \frac{e}{1 - \varrho_{xx}} \qquad (15)$$

In practice C_t will be of the order of 4 or 5 NCEs, ϱ_{xx} about 0.85; so that if our correction to the KR 20 of – 0.09 was out by $\pm 33\%$, we would be out in our estimate of $\bar{X}_{cs}$ by about one NCE or less.

Regressing Toward the Wrong Mean

Someone might suggest that instead of regarding our selection as being one of explicit restriction of a *school group*, we could perhaps treat it as explicit restriction of the *population*. This would of course greatly simplify our equation. Instead of equation (14), we would reformulate equation (12), thus:

$$\overline{X}_{cs} = \varrho_{xx}(\overline{X}_s - \mu_x) + \mu_x \qquad (16)$$

We could then take ϱ_{xx} directly from the publisher's tables, (or correct a KR 20), and, working directly in NCEs, we could put $\mu_x = 50$. Although there may be cases where this could yield reasonably accurate results, there is a flaw in the reasoning. The school group is the result of an implicit restriction of range of the population, for example, as a result of economic and housing pressures, followed by an explicit selection within the school. It can be shown that the two equations, (14) and (16), will yield identical results when, and *only* when

$$(\overline{X}_s - \mu_x) = \frac{\sigma^2}{s^2}(\overline{X}_s - \overline{X}_g) \qquad (17)$$

(Notice that equation [17] does not involve the reliability coefficient.)

In all other cases, the values will differ, and the result from equation (16) may be either larger than that from (14), or smaller; and one of the two must be incorrect. *The fallacy in the reasoning is the assumption that a subgroup must always regress to some larger population mean, however the sample is selected.* For example, if inaccurate measurement of height yields one group of Ituri forest pygmies and another of Watussi tribesmen, repeated measurements will simply produce regression to each group mean. Figure 5 should make the distinctions clear.

The outer ellipse represents the population bivariate distribution, and the inner one the group from which the selection is made. Both ellipses must be symmetrical about the common principal axis OA, since we assume the two tests to be parallel. $\overline{X}_s$, $\overline{X}_g$, and μ_x are the means of our selected sample, the group, and the population, respectively, and B and C are the centroids of the two ellipses, through each of which the appropriate regression lines pass. There is no constraint for these two lines to have the same slope, and in practice the group regression line is generally flatter than that for the population. If we correct assuming regression to the population mean, we will add the amount DF to the sample mean, whereas the appropriate correction will be the amount EF, regressing to the group mean. In this case, if the inner ellipse had appeared higher up the line OA, E would have fallen above D; and there would be a point between the two positions for which D and E would have coincided. At that point, equation (17) would apply.

It is even theoretically possible to divide a cut-off within a group or sample into separate homogeneous subgroups, each with its own mean for regression. Table 3 is a simulation of such a case. Notice that marginal distributions, shown at the bottom of the table below, give no clue of what is to follow; both are virtually normal. If we now apply equation (12) to the statistics of the ten selected pupils, we get

$$\overline{X}_{cs} = .8(30 - 50) + 50$$

$$= 34$$

**Figure 5. Correction to Group or Subpopulation Mean,
Versus Correction to Population Mean**

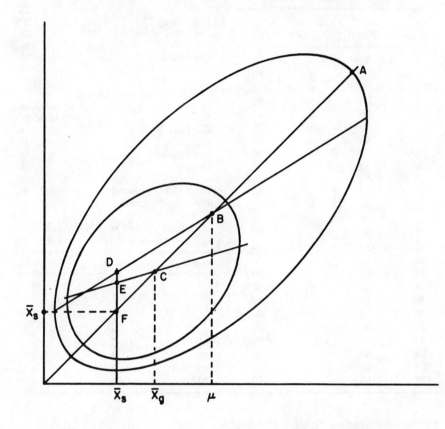

which is four points above the correct value of 30. The reason for the discrepancy can be seen in Figure 6. To dramatize the demonstration, there are no overlaps here between two very distinct groups; that is, when we divide into four quadrants, no cases appear in two of them. However, it is quite possible to have overlaps between groups, even though they regress to distinct means.

This has an important bearing on Title I studies, more particularly when the norm-referenced model is used. It is not suggested that Title I groups are dichotomously separated from the total population used for norming of tests, but the regulations governing their identification clearly create a subpopulation at least in terms of socioeconomic status of the school district. Title I students are selected from the subpopulation, not from the population. Therefore, as in Figure 6, the correct mean for regression will be the subpopulation mean. For additional reading see the now classic paper by Thorndike (1942, pp. 86, 101), and Campbell and Erlebacher (1970, p. 193). Furby (1973) is also a useful source.

Table 3. Example of Regression to Separate Means

Scores of Students on Tests 1 and 2

Pupil Number	Test 1	Selected Group	Test 2
1	50		60
2	20	x	40
3	30	x	30
4	60		50
5	30	x	40
6	50		70
7	40	x	30
8	20	x	10
9	70		50
10	50		50
11	60		80
12	40	x	20
13	40	x	40
14	80		60
15	50		60
16	10	x	20
17	70		50
18	60		50
19	70		70
20	30	x	30
21	60		60
22	90		90
23	40	x	40
24	80		70
25	50		70

Total Group

N	25
Test 1 Mean	50
Test 1 SD	20
Test 2 Mean	50
Test 2 SD 1	20
r	.8

Selected Group

Cut-off	40 and below
N	10 (40%)
Test 1 Mean	30
Test 1 SD	10
Test 2 Mean	30
Test 2 SD	10
r_{12}	.4
Test 2 Mean, predicted from overall regression	34

Frequency with Which Each Score Occurred on Tests 1 and 2

Score	Test 2	Test 1
10	1	1
20	2	2
30	3	3
40	4	4
50	5	5
60	4	4
70	3	3
80	2	2
90	1	1

Further Regression Toward the Mean

There is one last problem point which has persistently muddied the picture and led to much theoretical wrangling. It is the consequence of a failure to distinguish between the blanket concept of "Regression towards the mean," and the more restricted and specific application of this, the "Regression-effect bias." This makes it necessary to speak of "further regression towards the mean."

We can regard an individual test score (X) as being the sum of some real (even if composite) measure of an attribute (G), *plus* some individual variability (I) such as health, mood, attitude, motivation, and so on, *plus* the consequence of some deliberate intervention (S) by school or other source, *plus* the latitude (E) that performers are encouraged to find as a result of test format, for example, multiple choice, test design flaws, and so on, *plus* other sources. Thus

$$X_i = G_i + I_i + S_i + E_i + \ldots$$

Figure 6. Presence of Distinct Groups in a Combined Group

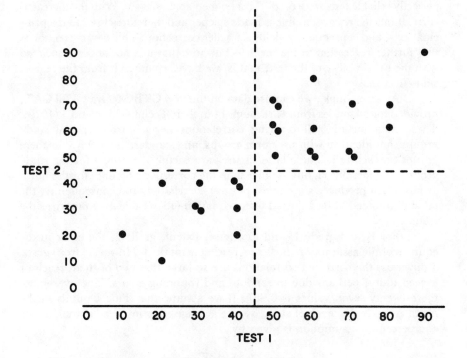

This is consistent with our earliest starting equations. It is not essential, but convenient, to regard the intercorrelations of the elements, with one exception, as being zero or close to it. It is also both convenient and necessary to lump I_i and E_i together (that is, to use two-occasion reliabilities) and regard them both as error. But it would be unreasonable to dismiss all other sources and retain only G_i and E_i. Real sources such as S_i must be allowed to remain, and here it is most unlikely that G_i and S_i will be uncorrelated.

In any case, the existence of additional sources of variance is no reason whatever why we should not make what allowance we can for E_i. What is left will account for any "further regression toward the mean"; it will also be the source of biases in such applications as the "equipercentile assumption" in the norm-referenced model. Here we have the situation referred to earlier in which we have both Galton's second real factor, *and* Gauss' error in each of two tests:

$$X_i = G_i + S_i + e_1$$

$$Y_i = G_i + T_i + e_2$$

One way of getting an indication of the amount of further regression which can disturb our equipercentile assumption is to correct the correlation for attenuation, and then to test the result for regression towards the mean.

Correcting for attenuation yields the correlation which would be obtained if perfectly reliable tests were used. Figure 6 then applies again. With the increased correlation, the regression line is made steeper and therefore closer to the principal axis, and consequently yields a smaller correction. This new correction is the "further regression to the mean"—but note that it is no longer associated with the unreliability of the test; that is, we have separated it from the regression-effect bias.

As an example, we can use data on the new CTB/McGraw-Hill CAT, provided for all grades from K through 11 in their Technical Bulletin 1 (1979). These data include fall-to-spring correlations derived from special study groups, not identical with the norm groups, and standard deviations for these groups on each test. These latter figures are useful; the ranges for the study group are generally slightly smaller than the corresponding ones for the norm group which produced the pretest-posttest correlation, and consequently, the reliabilities need to be adjusted using equation (13). Table 4 summarizes the results.

For K and grade 1, and to a lesser extent, grade 2, the error in the equipercentile assumption due to regression is marked. However, from grade 3 onwards, the corrected correlations are so large that two of them reach or exceed unity, perhaps due to random and rounding errors. The average of these twenty-seven values is 0.967. If we assume that Title I pupils in the norm group had a mean of about 34, the average error involved in making the equipercentile assumption is given by

$$\text{Error} = (1 - \varrho_{xx})(\overline{X}_s - \mu)$$

$$= (1 - 0.967)(34 - 50)$$

$$= -0.528 \text{ NCEs}$$

or about a half NCE too low; gains will be *overestimated* by this amount.

Discussion

When a test is made to serve two purposes simultaneously, namely the separation of a group into two distinct subgroups, as well as to provide an esti-

Table 4. Fall-Spring Correlations, Corrected for Attenutation

	K	1	2	3	4	Grades 5	6	7	8	9	10	11
Reading total	.83*	.84	.93	.95	(1.01)	.97	.99	.97	.98	.97	(1.03)	.97
Language total	—	—	.86	.92	.97	.96	.95	.96	.97	.95	.97	.96
Mathematics	.97	.83	.90	.91	.99	.93	.96	.97	.96	.96	.94	.98

*Total Prereading Skills
Note: Values in parentheses are overcorrections, possibly effects of random and rounding errors.

mate of the mean performance of one subgroup (or both of them), such estimates will be biased, generating appreciable error if not corrected. This bias is a direct consequence of the unreliability of the test used, the first effect being to misclassify individuals whose test scores were close enough to the cut-off value for errors of measurement to put them on the wrong side of that value. We will also have generated an important negative correlation between "true" scores and errors in both subgroups. This negative trend is not uniformly distributed, but has an increasing concentration as one approaches the cut-off value from either direction. We would underestimate the average performance level for the lower subgroup, and overestimate it for the upper. Retesting would restore the normal relationship of true scores to error.

Corrections can also be made on a theoretical-mathematical basis, although this calls for an estimate of the test reliability for the whole group — a correct figure being seldom available. In turn, we can estimate this figure if the reliability is known for the population. Publishers sometimes quote suitable figures, but often only Kuder-Richardson 20 or corrected split-half reliabilities are given, and these are unsuitable for our purposes; we need either alternate form, or retest reliabilities.

We can estimate the parameters we need, although our methods of estimation may introduce additional sources of error. Yet, our formula for correction of the regression effect bias is fairly robust.

There is always a danger that we may choose the wrong mean towards which we believe the subgroup will regress. But under no circumstances should we assume that the population mean can serve instead of the group mean, even though the temptation is great because of the simplicity of the resulting equation, and the easy availability of the statistics.

References

Boruch, R. F., and Creager, J. A. "Measurement Error in Social and Educational Survey Research." *ACE Research Reports,* May 1972, *7,* 1–50.

Burt, C. "Heredity and Environment." *Bulletin of the British Psychological Society,* 1971, *24,* 9–15.

Campbell, D. T., and Erlebacher, A. "How Regression Artifacts in Quasi-Experimental Evaluations Can Mistakenly Make Compensatory Education Look Harmful." In J. Hellmuth (Ed.), *Compensatory Education: A National Debate.* New York: Brunner-Mazel, 1970.

Cook, T. D., and Campbell, D. T. *Quasi-Experimentation: Design and Analysis for Field Settings.* Chicago: Rand McNally, 1976.

Cronbach, L. J., and Furby, L. "How We Should Measure 'Change' — Or Should We?" *Psychological Bulletin,* 1970, *74,* 68–80.

CTB/McGraw-Hill. *California Achievement Tests, Technical Bulletin 1.* Monterey, Calif.: CTB/McGraw-Hill, 1979.

English, H. B., and English, A. C. *A Comprehensive Dictionary of Psychological and Psycho-Analytical Terms.* New York: Longmans, Green, 1958.

Furby, L. "Interpreting Regression Toward the Mean in Developmental Research." *Developmental Psychology,* 1973, *8* (2), 172–179.

Galton, F. *Hereditary Genius.* Gloucester: Peter Smith, 1972. (Originally published 1869.)

Glass, G. *Regression Effect.* Memorandum, March 8, 1978.

Guilford, J. P. *Fundamental Statistics in Psychology and Education.* New York: McGraw-Hill, 1956.

Hays, W. L., and Winkler, R. L. *Statistics: Probability, Inference, and Decision.* New York: Holt, Rinehart and Winston, 1971.

Hopkins, K. D., and Glass, G. V. *Basic Statistics for the Behavioral Sciences.* Englewood Cliffs, N.J.: Prentice-Hall, 1978.

Humphreys, L. G. "To Understand Regression from Parent to Offspring, Think Statistically." *Psychological Bulletin,* 1978, *85* (6), 1317–1322.

Kenny, D. A. "A Quasi-Experimental Approach to Assessing Treatment Effects in the Non-Equivalent Control Group Design." *Psychological Bulletin,* 1975, *82* (3), 345–362.

Kirk, R. E. (Ed.). *Statistical Issues: A Reader for the Behavioral Sciences.* Monterey, Calif.: Brooks/Cole, 1972.

Levin, J. "Note on Effects of Restriction of Range on Reliability Coefficients." *Psychological Reports,* 1975, *36,* 115–118.

Overall, J. E., and Woodward, J. A. "Common Misconceptions Concerning the Analysis of Covariance." *Multivariate Behavioral Research,* April 1977, *12,* 171–186.

Overall, J. E., and Woodward, J. A. "Nonrandom Assignment and the Analysis of Covariance." *Psychological Bulletin,* 1977, *84* (3), 588–594.

Pearson, K. "Notes on the History of Correlation." *Biometrika,* 1920, *13,* 25–45.

Peters, C. C., and Van Voorhis, W. R. *Statistical Procedures and Their Mathematical Bases.* New York: McGraw-Hill, 1940.

Thorndike, R. L. "Regression Fallacies in the Matched Group Experiment." *Psychometrika,* 1942, *7,* 85–102.

Yule, G. U, and Kendall, N. G. *An Introduction to the Theory of Statistics.* London: Charles Griffin, 1950.

A. O. H. Roberts is a senior research associate at RMC Research Corporation, Mountain View, California.

*If the correlation between selection test and pretest is greater
than the correlation between selection test and posttest,
a selected group will continue to regress to the mean
in the norm-referenced model.*

Discussion:
Regression Toward the Mean
and the Interval Between
Test Administrations

Robert L. Linn

Roberts (this volume) has aptly observed that "'regression toward the mean' remains a source of argument, confusion, and error, despite seventy years of explanations, lay to didactic, kindly and otherwise." His own contribution clarifies some common confusions, but is unlikely to resolve one that is central to prevalent use of the norm-referenced model for Title I evaluations. The confusion that lacks satisfactory resolution is briefly addressed in the section of Roberts' chapter entitled "further regression toward the mean." The bulk of my comments will be focused on the issues which that section is intended to resolve.

Before addressing the issue of "further regression toward the mean," a few brief comments are in order about some of the other generally excellent contributions of Roberts' chapter. The specification of the effects that selection on observed scores has on the correlation between true scores and error scores is quite enlightening. The specific equations for the regression of error on true score and for the correlation between error and true scores in the selected groups are not generally available and are very informative. His Figure 3, which shows the nonlinear form of the regression of error on true scores, is also instructive.

Other aspects of Roberts' paper which seem particularly noteworthy are the sections on historical background and on the distinction among types of reliability coefficients. It is fascinating, although somewhat discouraging, to see the parallels between contemporary and historical interpretations. The caution that "reliability coefficients are created unequal," while hardly a new insight, is important and too often overlooked with internal consistency coefficients inappropriately used in situations where alternate form coefficients are needed.

Posttest Versus Pretest Regression on Selection Test

1. Roberts' Disattenuated Correlation Approach. Despite the positive contributions of Roberts' chapter, it does not deal adequately with an issue that is fundamental to the validity of the norm-referenced model for Title I evaluation. This is the concern, which to my knowledge was first raised by Glass (1978), that the correlation between the posttest and the selection test is apt to be less than the correlation between the pretest and the selection test. If so, a selected group will show greater regression toward the mean on the posttest than on the pretest and therefore yield a biased estimate of the effect of Title I.

Roberts considers this argument somewhat indirectly under the heading "further regression toward the mean." Disattenuated correlations between fall and spring CAT scores are reported in Table 4 of his chapter. He argues that these disattenuated correlations, with the exception of the ones for grades K, 1, and 2, are so high that the amount of *overestimation* of the effect of Title I due to this source of error will be quite small. Indeed, using the average disattenuated correlation of .967 for the 27 grade-3-and-above-values and a Title I mean NCE of 34, he estimates that the bias due to this error is only about 0.5 NCE units.

Disattentuated correlations have several disadvantages including large sampling errors and the embarrassment of obtaining values greater than 1.0, as happened twice in Table 4. Their value also depends on the appropriateness of the reliability estimates that are used to "correct" the correlation. Roberts does not explain what type of reliabilities were used, but does note that they come from the norm group and had to be adjusted for differences in standard deviations between the norm group and the special study groups for which fall-spring correlations were available. This adjustment adds noise to the estimates. Furthermore, as will be demonstrated later, there is no need to rely upon reliability estimates and disattenuated correlations. Observed correlations are all that is required.

Before considering a more direct approach, it is worth noting that even relying on the disattenuated correlations in Table 4 of Roberts' chapter, one might reasonably conclude that the bias in the early grades is sometimes unacceptably large. The average of the 10 disattenuated correlations for grades K through 3 in Roberts' Table 4 is .894. Using Roberts' approach, the amount of bias for Title I pupils with a mean of 34 is given by $(1.0 - 0.894)(34 - 50) =$ -1.696 NCE's. In other words, gains for Title I would be *overestimated* by about 1.7 NCE's based on this average disattenuated correlation. In the worst case (grade 1 math or K reading), the disattenuated correlation is .83 and the corresponding bias for Title I pupils with a mean of 34 is 2.72 NCE's, an amount that can hardly be ignored in light of experience with the magnitude of estimated Title I effects.

More important than quibbles over whether estimates based on Roberts' Table 4 suggest acceptably small bias or unacceptably large bias is the fact that they are only suggestive. A small disattenuated correlation does not necessarily imply unequal regression of posttest and of pretest on the selection test. Two variables which have only a modest correlation with each other could have identical correlations with a third variable (in this case the selection test). Even a disattenuated correlation of 1.0 is inconclusive without knowledge of the pretest and posttest reliabilities. If the reliabilities are unequal then the observed scores on the pretest and on the posttest will have unequal correlations with a third variable, and therefore unequal regression effects, despite a disattenuated correlation of 1.0. The latter is only suggestive: a more direct evaluation is needed.

2. **Direct Approach.** As already indicated, it is not necessary to use reliabilities and disattenuated correlations. One need not even invoke the concept of errors of measurement. As stated by Humphreys (1978), "Regression is a statistical phenomenon" (p. 1317). Errors of measurement are only one possible interpretation. The key to understanding the possible bias due to regression in the norm-referenced model depends only on a consideration of the relative magnitudes of the correlations between pairs of tests involved in the model. The following argument would apply equally well to measures that were free of errors of measurement (or essentially so, such as the weight example used by Lord, 1967). All that is required is that the correlations between pairs of measures be less than 1.0 and of unequal value.

The norm-referenced model requires a selection test, S, a pretest, X, and a posttest, Y. By selecting on S and then estimating the effect of Title I by comparing the mean NCE on X to the mean NCE on Y it was hoped that the bias due to the Title I students regressing toward the mean would be eliminated. I have previously argued that the model requirement that selection be based on S rather than X "is helpful because the pretest as well as the posttest will display a regression toward the mean . . . [but] the regression effect for the posttest will *not* equal the regression effect for the pretest unless the selection measure has the *same* correlation with the posttest as it does with the pretest" (emphasis added) (Linn, 1979, p. 26). This is the basis of the criticism by Glass (1978) which seems to be somewhat obscured by Roberts' treatment of his argument.

Is the correlation between S and X equal to the correlation between S and Y? This is a simple empirical question, but one which, despite the substantial resources that are devoted to Title I evaluations and to evaluation models, has apparently not been adequately dealt with. Since the time interval between S and X is less than the one between S and Y, one would certainly expect the correlation between S and Y to be less than the one between S and X, and therefore for there to be a larger regression effect on the posttest than on the pretest. Thus, one would expect that there would be some bias in the direction of overestimating the effect of Title I due to greater regression on Y than on X.

Suppose, for example, that S, X and Y are all reported in NCE units (that is, have means of 50 and standard deviations of 21.06) for some norm group and S correlates .9 with X and .8 with Y. Further suppose that the mean on S for students selected for Title I is 34. In the absence of any effect of Title I, the expected means on X and Y are:

$$50 + (.9)(34 - 50) = 35.6, \text{ and}$$

$$50 + (.8)(34 - 50) = 37.2.$$

In other words there would be a bias of 1.6 NCE (that is, 37.2 – 35.6) in the estimated effect of Title I. Note that no assumptions about errors of measurement, parallel measures or reliability are required.

The natural question is whether the correlations of S with X and S with Y are usually more or less similar than in the above example. Unfortunately, this question is not well answered. Results from the Sustaining Effects Study (Hemenway, Wang, Kenoyer, Hoepfner, Bear, and Smith, 1978) can be used to shed some light on the question, however. The typical pattern of testing for the norm-referenced Title I model is to administer S in the spring, select students for Title I programs for the following academic year during which X is administered in the fall and Y in the spring. Thus, there is a spring-fall-spring testing pattern in the typical application. The relevant correlations are therefore between a test given the spring and one the following fall for S with X and a test given in the spring with one the following spring for S and Y.

Hemenway and others (1978) reported test-retest correlations for fall to spring, spring to fall, and fall to fall. While the testing pattern does not exactly match the desired pattern, it does provide a comparison of correlations between tests administered in the spring and the following fall and ones given with several months of instruction intervening (fall to spring) or a year apart (fall to fall). The average correlations reported by Hemenway and others (1978) are listed in Table 1. Averages were taken over different sequences of levels of the test. For example, in grades one through two, levels A, B, and C of the CTBS were used with 590 students taking levels in the sequence ABB, 595 in sequence ABC, and 600 in sequence ACC for the fall-spring-fall test administrations. As shown in Table 1, the total number of students for the grade-one-to-two average was 1785.

The spring-to-fall correlations are larger in every case than either the corresponding fall-to-spring or fall-to-fall correlation. Correlations for the latter two periods are remarkably similar. The differences in the magnitude of the spring-to-fall correlations and the ones for the other two time intervals are larger in the early grades than in the later grades, a finding that is consistent with Roberts' disattenuated correlation results based on his Table 4.

To get an indication of the likely magnitude of the bias caused by a smaller correlation between S and Y than between S and X, the spring-1-to-fall-2 average correlations were used as estimates of the correlation of S with X

Table 1. Average Test-Retest Correlations for the Debiased CTBS
Scales (based on Hemenway and others, 1978, p. 47)

Cohort/ Grade	Total N	Spring 1 Fall 2	Fall 1 Spring 1	Fall 1 Fall 2
		Reading		
1−2	1785	.80	.59	.59
2−3	1794	.84	.76	.77
3−4	1497	.87	.81	.82
4−5	1761	.85	.81	.83
5−6	1608	.90	.88	.88
		Math		
1−2	1785	.70	.62	.61
2−3	1794	.74	.67	.70
3−4	1497	.79	.71	.72
4−5	1761	.79	.73	.75
5−6	1608	.81	.77	.77
		Basic Skills		
1−2	1785	.82	.69	.69
2−3	1794	.85	.79	.81
3−4	1497	.88	.82	.83
4−5	1761	.88	.84	.85
5−6	1608	.90	.88	.88

for each achievement area and grade. The average of the fall-1-to-spring-1 and fall-1-to-fall-2 correlations was used in place of the correlation of S with Y. NCE scales were then assumed for each test. For means on S of 25 and 34, which are intended to simulate possible means for groups selected for Title I programs, the expected means on X and Y were computed. For example, for cohort/grades one to two in reading the expected pretest and posttest means are respectively

$$50 + (.80)(25 - 50) = 30, \text{ and}$$

$$50 + (.59)(25 - 50) = 35.25$$

when the mean on S is 25. The bias, that is, the amount by which the Title I treatment effect is *overestimated*, is simply the difference between an expected posttest and pretest means. For the above example the bias is 5.25 NCE's.

The expected pretest and posttest means and the bias in NCE units is reported in Table 2 for each test and cohort and each assumed mean on the selection for Title I students. There is a fairly consistent tendency for the bias to be larger in the early grades, especially for cohort/grade one to two, and smaller for the higher grades. In every instance there is some bias in the direction of overestimating the effect of Title I. Since the results are based on a linear model, the bias is naturally greater for a more severely selected group (mean S of 25 in the example) than for a less severely selected group (mean S of 34 in the example).

Table 2. Expected Pretest and Posttest Means and Expected Bias in Title I Estimated Effect (Based on Correlations from Table 1)

Cohort/ Grade	Mean on S = 25			Mean on S = 34		
	Expected Pretest Mean	Expected Posttest Mean	Bias	Expected Pretest Mean	Expected Posttest Mean	Bias
			Reading			
1–2	30.00	35.35	5.25	37.20	40.56	3.36
2–3	29.00	30.88	1.88	36.56	37.76	1.20
3–4	28.25	29.62	1.37	36.08	36.96	.88
4–5	28.75	29.50	.70	36.40	36.88	.48
5–6	27.50	28.00	.50	35.60	35.92	.32
			Math			
1–2	32.50	34.62	2.12	38.80	40.16	1.36
2–3	31.50	32.88	1.38	38.16	39.04	.88
3–4	30.25	32.12	1.87	37.36	38.56	1.20
4–5	30.25	31.50	1.25	37.36	38.16	.80
5–6	29.75	30.75	1.00	37.04	37.68	.64
			Basic Skills			
1–2	29.50	32.75	3.25	36.88	38.96	2.08
2–3	28.75	30.00	1.25	36.40	37.20	.80
3–4	28.00	29.38	1.38	35.92	36.80	.88
4–5	28.00	28.88	.88	35.92	36.48	.56
5–6	27.50	28.00	.50	35.60	35.92	.32

Some people may consider bias of the magnitude illustrated in Table 2 to be intolerably large, while others may find it acceptably small. In any event, the magnitude, in the early grades at least, is sufficient that it cannot reasonably be ignored. It is clear that the requirement of selecting on a test other than the pretest reduces but does not eliminate the bias in estimating the effect of Title I that is due to regression toward the mean.

The results in Tables 1 and 2 apply to only one test and are not based upon quite the right pattern of test results. Thus, they can hardly be considered definitive. They do provide a rather strong indication that a problem remains and may provide fairly reasonable estimates of the likely magnitude of the problem. If the norm-referenced model is to continue to be widely used, better estimates of the correlations between S and X and between S and Y are needed for the most commonly used testing patterns and most commonly used tests.

References

Glass, G. V. *Regression Effect.* Memorandum, March 8, 1978.

Hemenway, J. A., Wang, M., Kenoyer, C. E., Hoepfner, R., Bear, M. B., and Smith, G. *The Measures and Variables in the Sustaining Effects Study.* Report 9. Santa Monica, Calif.: Systems Development Corp., 1978.

Humphreys, L. G. "Investigations of the Simplex." *Psychometrika,* 1969, *25,* 313-323.

Humphreys, L. G. "To Understand Regression from Parent to Offspring, Think Statistically." *Psychological Bulletin,* 1978, *85,* 1317-1322.

Linn, R. L. "Validity of Inferences Based on the Proposed Title I Evaluation Models." *Educational Evaluation and Policy Analysis,* 1979, *1,* 23-32.

Lord, F. M. "A Paradox in the Interpretation of Group Comparison." *Psychological Bulletin,* 1967, *68,* 304-305.

*Robert L. Linn is professor of educational psychology
at the University of Illinois, Urbana.*

*In Roberts' chapter the regression effect was discussed
using a two-variable model while the norm-referenced
model relies on three test administrations.*

Discussion:
Underlying Assumptions
and Resulting Biases

Robert S. Burton

The Title I Evaluation and Reporting System (TIERS) has been designed to estimate the effect of Title I treatment on the achievement test scores of participating students. Three procedures have been developed for this purpose, one of which has attracted much attention, both for its wide acceptance at the district level and for its questionable theoretical status. This is Model A, also known as the norm-referenced model, since it uses test publishers' national norming samples as surrogates for local control or comparison groups.

The description of Model A can be found in Tallmadge and Wood (1978). In summary, it is a three-test procedure: Students are selected on the basis of scoring below a cutoff point on Test 1 (Model A does not require use of a norm-referenced test for selection; the great majority of districts, however, do base selection on such a test), are retested prior to treatment with Test 2, and are tested after treatment with Test 3. All test scores are expressed in a metric that is nationally normed and normally distributed at each point in time. The treatment effect is defined, for any Title I group, as the difference between the observed mean score on Test 3 and the expected mean score, or no-treatment expectation, on Test 3. The problem, of course, is to determine a no-treatment expectation that is both theoretically sound and amenable to calculation at the local level.

The Model A solution to this problem is elegant in its simplicity: Assume that the expected score on Test 3 is equal to the observed score on Test 2. Burton (1979) has noted that this does not define a model in any usual sense of the word, but only a computational procedure. There is no nomological network or set of linkages among the three test scores; in short, no underlying structure has been advanced that would lead to the Model A assumption.

The main purpose of this chapter is to develop the model that underlies the procedure known as Model A. The assumptions of this model will be made explicit, as will the biases to which they lead. The results will be developed and presented in a general statistical framework, and will then be reformulated in psychometric terms, in an attempt to bridge the large gap between the present mode of discourse and that used by Roberts (this volume). Finally, some general remarks will be presented on the relative merits of two-test and three-test models.

The Relevance of Roberts' Work to Model A

It is difficult to relate Roberts' (this volume) arguments to the validity of Model A, since he presents no model based on three test administrations. He chooses, instead, to discuss various aspects of a two-test procedure, and to introduce a third test only tangentially. For the purposes of this chapter, Roberts' position seems to be summarized in the following paragraph:

> On retesting each of these two groups with a test which has no other basis than true score for correlation with the first, however, the absence of any new barriers allows the independence of true score and error score to reassert itself. The resulting means will represent the unbiased estimates of the mean ability of each group. This fact has considerable significance: *Selection based on observed test score is a source of bias; and all bias from this source disappears at the first new test for which there is no new constraint from selection.* Note that we have not abolished random error; we have merely banished the bias that resulted from selected errors.

There are four points of interest in this passage: Two are substantive, and two methodological.

First, to begin with substantive issues, it is not a "fact" that the second test "has no other basis than true score for correlation with the first," nor is it a "fact" that administration of a second test "allows the independence of true score and error score to reassert itself." These are unsupported assumptions. In the context of Model A, they will be shown to be untenable. Second, while it is true that "we have not abolished random error," it is also true that the Model A computational procedure assumes that we have abolished it. This too will be demonstrated.

Third, to move to methodological issues, it is not clear why one would attach "considerable significance" to statements — whether true or false — relating to the extent of bias in Test 2 scores insofar as they estimate true scores. Model A does not depend on estimating true scores. It depends on estimating observed scores in Test 3, and, for this purpose, observed scores on Test 2 provide a biased estimate.

The fourth issue is related to the third, and is central to the approach taken in Roberts' chapter. The reliance on dissection of observed scores into true and error components is metaphysical in its intensity, as when it is announced that "our recognition restores Gauss's 'error' to the central position from which Galton has evicted it." But the validity of the psychometric approach cannot be grounded in the reification of error scores; Kenny (1979) has noted that "rather than choosing one's specifications by one's discipline, specifications should be chosen to fit the problem" (p. 23). (He also observed that "what sets aside psychometrics from other statistical approaches is the almost excessive concern about measurement error"[p. 74].) Psychometric methods are useful if they clarify, and not useful if they obscure. In the present case, they serve mainly to obscure.

Two Equations for No-Treatment Expectation

The Model A assumption is that if the mean scores are known for the first two test administrations, the no-treatment expectation for the third test administration is equal to the obtained score on the second administration. There is no compelling reason to express this assumption in terms of true scores and error scores. It is a statement about an expected value, namely:

$$E(\overline{X}_3|\overline{X}_1, \overline{X}_2) = \overline{X}_2 \tag{1}$$

On the other hand, Echternacht (1978) has noted that the general formulation for this conditional expectation, assuming that only scores are randomly selected from a trivariate normal distribution, is given by:

$$E(\overline{X}_3|\overline{X}_1, \overline{X}_2) = \frac{\sigma_{13} - \sigma_{12}\sigma_{23}}{1 - \sigma_{12}^2}\overline{X}_1 + \frac{\sigma_{23} - \sigma_{12}\sigma_{13}}{1 - \sigma_{12}^2}\overline{X}_2 \tag{2}$$

(It is assumed, without loss of generality, that $\mu_i = 0$, $\sigma_{ij} = 1$, for $i = 1,2,3$; it follows that σ_{ij}, $i = j$, represents a test-retest reliability between administration i and administration j.)

Three conclusions follow immediately. First, equation (2) is completely general, depending only on the assumption of trivariate normality; it is difficult to think of any reasonable alternative assumption. Second, equations (1) and (2) generally yield different expected values for $\overline{X}_3$; more specifically, given the value of $\overline{X}_1$, there is one and only one value for $\overline{X}_2$ such that (1) is consistent with (2). Third, setting arithmetic aside for a moment, the absence of $\overline{X}_1$ on the right-hand side of (1) violates common sense: surely, knowledge of $\overline{X}_1$ should influence the prediction of $\overline{X}_3$.

Echternacht concluded that Model A is generally invalid. Our goal is to pursue this invalidity to its source, by explicitly stating the assumptions that are required to transform equation (2) into equation (1).

Assumptions Behind Model A

The passage from the general equation to the Model A equation turns out to be simple and direct. First, in order to eliminate one of the two variables, $\overline{X}_1$ and $\overline{X}_2$, from equation (2), it is necessary to hypothesize a deterministic relationship between them. The obvious choice is the hypothesis that the observed value of $\overline{X}_2$ is equal to its expected value given $\overline{X}_1$:

$$\overline{X}_2 = E(\overline{X}_2|\overline{X}_1) = \sigma_{12}\overline{X}_1. \tag{3}$$

Solving (3) for $\overline{X}_1$ and substituting in (2) yields:

$$E(\overline{X}_3|\overline{X}_1,\ \overline{X}_2) = \frac{\sigma_{13}}{\sigma_{12}}\overline{X}_2 \tag{4}$$

which is quite similar to equation (1). Again, the necessary hypothesis is obvious: assume that $\sigma_{13} = \sigma_{12}$. Substitution into (4) then produces the Model A no-treatment expectation.

To summarize, the Model A computational procedure is equivalent to the following three assumptions:

- Mean scores on the selection test, pretest, and posttest have a joint distribution that is trivariate normal (A1)
- The observed mean score on the pretest is equal to its expected value given the observed mean on the selection test (A2)
- The correlation between selection test scores and pretest scores is equal to the correlation between selection test scores and posttest scores (A3)

The dependence of Model A on assumption A3 has been noted previously (Glass, 1978); the relationship between Model A and assumption A2 does not seem to have been explicitly stated by previous critics. Both assumptions are unrealistic, and lead to biased no-treatment expectations.

Implications of Model A Assumptions

Glass (1978) has observed that test-retest reliabilities decay over time, so that the only reasonable assumption regarding the relative sizes of σ_{12} and σ_{13} is that $\sigma_{12} > \sigma_{13}$, or $\sigma_{12} - \sigma_{13} > 0$. It follows from equation (4) that $E(\overline{X}_3|\overline{X}_1,\ \overline{X}_2) > \overline{X}_2$, so that assumption A3 leads to a no-treatment expectation that is negatively biased and a treatment effect that is positively biased. The extent of the bias depends on the particular test, the population from which the Title I group is drawn, and the elapsed times between test administrations. The bias is probably small. Since *any* positive treatment effect is considered good, however, *any* negative bias in the no-treatment expectation should be considered serious.

Assumption A2 introduces an entirely different problem. It leads to a bias which, for a particular Title I group, may be either positive or negative, depending on the deviation of $\overline{X}_2$ from its expected value; the smaller the group, the more likely that the deviation is large in absolute value. When data are aggregated across projects, the expected deviation will be very close to zero. On the one hand, this is the basic function of Model A. On the other hand, districts are told that Model A results can be utilized at the local level, for example, for comparisons among classrooms. This is bad advice, and should not be promulgated.

Model A Assumptions Expressed in Terms of Error Scores

Although the properties of Model A are best explored in statistical terms, it may be of interest to translate the results into the terminology of measurement theory. Toward this end, consider the decomposition of observed scores into their true and error components, given by $X_i = t + e_i$, $i = 1,2,3$, and note that σ_{ij} is equal to the covariance of X_i and X_j. The difference, $\sigma_{12} - \sigma_{13}$, can then be expanded and expressed as:

$$\sigma_{12} - \sigma_{13} = Cov(t, e_2) - Cov(t, e_3) + Cov(e_1, e_2) - Cov(e_1, e_3) \qquad (5)$$

In classical theory, as espoused by Roberts, all four terms on the right-hand side of (5) are assumed to vanish.

Since there is empirical evidence that $\sigma_{12} - \sigma_{13} > 0$, the classical theory is inappropriate: either true scores remain correlated with error scores, or error scores are correlated with one another over time, or both. The most reasonable hypothesis is that error sources have varying half-lives, implying that $Cov(e_1, t) > Cov(e_2, t) > Cov(e_3, t) > 0$, and that $Cov(e_1, e_3) > 0$.

The above remarks may shed some light on the status of assumption A3. It is, of course, irrelevant whether we attribute the bias produced by this assumption to "further regression to the mean" or to "regression effect bias"; the important fact is that it exists. Assumption A2 is dealt with more easily, since it can be reduced to the hypothesis that e_2 assumes its expected value, that is, $e_2 = E(e_2)$. Although it seems obvious, it apparently bears restating that this assumption only applies to "an infinite number of individuals" (Magnusson, 1966, p. 64).

Alternatives to the Model A Assumptions

Since assumptions A2 and A3 lead to biased estimates, it is appropriate to return to the more general formulation given by equation (2). This provides an unbiased estimate of the no-treatment expectation, but has the unfortunate disadvantage of requiring knowledge of three test-retest correlations. It would be preferable to find other assumptions that produce little or no bias, while not imposing additional computational burdens on school and district staff.

It might be reasonable to assume that $\sigma_{12} = \sigma_{23}$, if selection and pretesting are close in time, and if they utilize either the same test or two very similar tests. This leads to:

$$E(\overline{X}_3 | \overline{X}_1, \overline{X}_2) = \frac{\sigma_{13}}{1 - \sigma_{12}} (\overline{X}_1 + \overline{X}_2), \qquad (6)$$

which still requires knowledge of two correlations. If we take the final step in this direction, and assume that all three correlations are equal, we arrive at:

$$E(\overline{X}_3|\overline{X}_1,\ \overline{X}_2) = \frac{\sigma}{1-\sigma}(\overline{X}_1 + \overline{X}_2), \tag{7}$$

where σ denotes the one "typical" correlation that must be estimated. In neither of these cases is assumption A2 necessary; this is a definite advantage.

Closer examination of equations (6) and (7) reveals that they essentially define a two-test design, since $\overline{X}_1$ and $\overline{X}_2$ appear only in the form of a sum. This design would involve selecting students on the basis of scores obtained on the first half of a pretest, and then administering the second half of that test to the selected students. (It should be noted that the right-hand side of equation (7) can be interpreted as the Spearman-Brown correction factor for doubling the test length, applied to the mean of the two test scores.) Both equations introduce some bias, require knowledge of at least one test-retest correlation for a local subpopulation, and still necessitate three test administrations. In short, they have little to recommend them. The conclusion to be drawn is that there does not appear to be any three-test procedure that is both easily implemented and theoretically superior to Model A.

Conclusion: The Usefulness of Model A

The preceding section reveals the one major advantage of Model A: it is the only norm-referenced evaluation procedure (for groups chosen on the basis of extreme scores) that requires no data other than the test scores themselves. On the debit side, it introduces two sources of bias and involves three test administrations.

The only viable alternative to Model A is the two-test procedure discussed by Roberts and others. It offers the advantages of less bias and less testing. It does necessitate, however, as Roberts has stressed, use of the subpopulation mean and test-retest reliability. Whether it would, in practice, produce more valid information than Model A is not clear. In choosing one of the two procedures, it is important to understand the underlying models, and to be aware of the advantages and disadvantages of each.

References

Burton, R. S. *Longitudinal Norm-Referenced Evaluation: The Search for a Model.* Paper presented at annual meeting of the American Educational Research Association, San Francisco, April 1979.

Echternacht, G. Memorandum, April 24, 1978.

Glass, G. V. *Regression Effect.* Memorandum, March 8, 1978.

Kenny, D. *Correlation and Causality.* New York: Wiley, 1979.

Magnusson, D. *Test Theory.* Reading, Mass.: Addison-Wesley, 1966.

Tallmadge, G. K., and Wood, C. T. *User's Guide.* Mountain View, Calif.: RMC Research Corp., 1978.

Robert S. Burton is a technical manager with Applied Management Sciences, Inc., in Silver Spring, Maryland.

Index

A

American Educational Research Association (AERA), vii, 11, 45, 47, 49
American Institutes for Research, 3
American Psychological Association, 45, 47, 49
Anchor Test Study (ATS), 38
Anderson, J. I., 4, 16, 26, 29
Angoff, W. H., 38, 49
Appelbaum, W. R., 40, 49
Armor, D., 21, 23, 28
Arter, J. A., viii, 17–31

B

Baker, R., 21, 28
Barker, P., 39, 50, 56, 58
Bear, M. B., 86, 88
Beaton, A., Jr., 23, 30
Belmont data collection system, 3
Belsen, W. A., 6, 15
Bessey, B., 4, 15
Bianchini, J. C., 38, 50
Binkley, J., 3, 15
Bland, J. D., 16, 22, 23, 31
Boldt, R. F., 42, 49
Boruch, R. F., 26, 28, 65, 81
Bridgemann, B., 21, 28
Bureau of Elementary and Secondary Education, 3
Burstein, L., 21, 28
Burt, C., 61–62, 81
Burton, B., 19, 22, 28
Burton, R. S., viii, 91–96

C

California Achievement Test (CAT), 14, 39, 80, 84
California Reading Test, 43
California Test of Basic Skills (CTBS), 86, 87
Campbell, D. J., 59, 60, 77, 81
Campbell, D. T., 18, 19, 20, 24, 28, 31, 60, 81
Campbell, E. Q., 28
Carter, L., 8, 12, 15
Cech, J., 23, 28

Chance-level scores: alternative approaches to, 53–54; assessing reliability and validity of, 51–54; correlational assessments of, 41, 42–43; distributional assessments of, 41–42, 43; and examinee behavior, 51–53; and internal consistency, 42, 43–44; randomness of, 41–44; responsibility for evaluation of, 45, 46–48; Title I example of, 44–46; usefulness of, 55–57
Chiang, A., 4, 15
Cliff, R., 42, 49
Cochran, W., 6, 15
Coleman, J. S., 23, 28
College Board, 42
Compensatory rivalry, 19, 27
Conklin, J. E., 21, 28
Conry-Oseguera, P., 28
Control group model. *See* Model B
Cook, T. D., 18, 24, 28, 60, 81
Coombs, C. H., 52, 54
Cooper, M. L., 16, 23, 31
Cox, M., 28
Crane, L. R., 23, 28, 31
Creager, J. A., 65, 81
Cronbach, L. J., 19, 28, 60, 81
Cross, C., 9–10, 15
Crowder, C. R., 21, 28
Crowe, M. B., 23, 31
CTB/McGraw-Hill, 80, 81

D

Dallas Independent School District, 40
Data, empirical, smoothing and fitting of, in Model A, 21–22
David, J. L., 21, 28
DeGracie, J. S., 26, 28
Demoralization, resentful: defined, 19; and Model C., 27
DeVito, P. J., 21, 24, 28, 30
Doherty, W., 23, 29, 39, 49, 56, 58
Donlon, T. F., viii, 33–50, 51, 54, 55–56
Dressel, P. L., 52, 54

E

Ebel, R. L., 52, 54
Echternacht, G. J., vii–viii, 1–16, 19, 22, 29, 33, 49, 93, 96

Educational Testing Service (ETS), 4, 9, 13
Elementary and Secondary Education Act (ESEA), Title I of: and chance-level scores, 44–46; and compensatory education, vii, 8; Section 124 (g) of, 1
English, A. C., 62, 81
English, H. B., 62, 81
Equipercentile function, and Model A, 21, 34
Erlebacher, A., 59, 60, 77, 81
Estes, G. D., 21, 22, 23, 26, 28, 29
Evaluation: changing approaches to, 3–4, 13–15; distrust of, 2, 10; by functional-level testing, 33–50; history of, 2–4; intervals in, and regression, 83–89; legislation on, 1–2, 10, 11; problems of, 2–3, 12; program consolidation for, 14; record of, vii; and reports to Congress, 11–13; requirements for, 4; use of information from, 15
Evaluation models: common features of, 33; described, 5–7; development of, 1–16; internal validity of, 17–31; issues of, 9–11; normed and nonnormed, 7; premises of, 4–5; school district use of, 7–9. *See also* Model A; Model B; Model C
Extrapolation, and Model A, 21

F

Faddis, B. J., 18, 21, 22, 23, 29, 30
Fagan, B., 12, 16
Fipe, D., 16
Fischer, F. E., 43–44, 49
Fishbein, R. L., 24, 29
Flaugher, R. L., 43, 50
Floor effects: identifying, 36; in widely used tests, 37
Florida, NCE gains in, 8
Fowler, H. M., 43, 49
Frechtling, J. A., 22, 23, 29
Friendly, L. P., 21, 29
Fuentes, E. J., 21, 29
Functional-level testing: and chance-level scores, 41–44; criteria for, 33–50; current guidelines for, 35–37; defined, 34; guidelines for, recommended, 34–35, 48–49; and motivational effects, 55–58; and out-of-level testing, 37–41; and reliability, 35–36
Furby, L., 60, 77, 81

G

Gallas, E. J., 21, 31
Galton, F., 59, 60–61, 62, 63, 64, 71, 79, 81, 93
Gamel, N., 3, 15
Gates McGinnitie tests, 39
Gauss, K. F., 61, 62, 63, 79, 93
Gladney, M. B., 42, 49
Glass, G. V., 22, 29, 60, 64, 81, 82, 84, 85, 88, 94, 96
Goldberger, A. S., 29
Graduate Record Examination, 44
Green, D. R., 43, 50
Guilford, J. P., 36, 49, 74, 82
Gulliksen, H., 36, 45, 49

H

Haenn, J. F., 21, 29
Hammond, D. C., 29
Hammond, P. A., 22, 23, 29
Hardy, R. A., 8, 15, 21, 29
Harvey, P., 23, 31
Hays, W. L., 60, 82
Hemenway, J. A., 86, 87, 88
Hendrickson, G., 1, 2, 15
Hepworth, D. H., 29
Hills, J. R., 42–43, 49
Hiscox, S. B., 21, 22, 23, 25, 29
History: defined, 18; local, 19; and Model A, 20; and Model B, 24; and selection, 25
Hobson, C. J., 28
Hoepfner, R., 86, 88
Holthouse, N. D., 21–22, 23, 25, 29
Hoover, H. D., 39, 40, 50
Hopkins, K. D., 37, 49, 60, 82
Horst, D. P., 21, 31
Horwitz, S., 24, 26, 30
House, G. D., 23, 29
Humphreys, L. G., 60, 82, 85, 89
Hunter, E. L., 16, 23, 31

I

Influence, ambiguity about direction of, 19
Instrumentation: defined, 18; and Model A, 20–21; and Model B, 24; and Model C, 26; and selection, 23, 25
Internal validity: of Model A, 19–23, 27–28; of Model B, 24–25, 27; of Model C, 25–27; threats to, 18–19; of TIERS, 17–31

Interpolation, and Model A, 21
Iowa Tests of Basic Skills, 39

J

Jaeger, R. M., 11, 15, 21, 29
Jeffress, E. L., 21, 29
Johnson, L. B., vii
Johnson, M. L., 23, 31

K

Kaskowitz, D. H., 21, 23, 25, 29-30
Keesling, J. W., 21, 28
Kellogg, T. M., 21, 30, 39, 50, 56, 58
Kendall, N. G., 60, 82
Kennedy, R., 1
Kenny, D. A., 6, 7, 15, 60, 82, 93, 96
Kenoyer, C. E., 86, 88
King, N., 28
Kirk, R. E., 82
Klibanoff, L. S., 24, 30

L

Laplace, P. S., 61
Levin, J., 67, 82
Levine, M. V., 44, 49
Levine, R. D., 43, 49
Linn, R. L., viii, 21, 23, 25, 30, 31, 38-39, 40, 49, 50, 83-89
Long, J. V., 21, 24, 26, 28, 30, 39, 49-50, 56, 58
Lord, F. M., 39, 43, 49, 50, 85, 89
Loret, P. G., 38, 50
Loyd, B. H., 39, 40, 50

M

McDonnell, P., 28
McLaughlin, M., 1, 15
McNemar, Q., 6, 15
McPartland, J., 28
MacRae, P. J., 43, 50
Magnusson, D., 95, 96
Mandeville, G. K., 22, 30
Maturation: defined, 18; and Model A, 20; and Model B, 24; and Model C, 26; and selection, 25, 27
Mayeske, G. W., 23, 30
Metropolitan Achievement Test (MAT), 21, 23, 39, 45
Michaels, P., 16
Milholland, J. E., 52, 54

Model A: alternative assumptions for, 95-96; assumptions behind, 93-94; changes in, 14; described, 5-6; equivalent scores in, 40; and error scores, 95; implementation of, 34; implications of assumptions in, 94-95; internal validity of, 19-23, 27-28; issues of, 10; no-treatment expectation in, 19, 93; and Roberts' work, 92-93; as three-test procedure, 91-92; use of, 33; usefulness of, 96
Model B: described, 6; history of, 19; internal validity of, 24-25, 27; use of, 7-8
Model C: described, 6-7; experience with, 8-9; history of, 19; internal validity of, 25-27; issues of, 11
Mood, A. M., 28
Morris, S., 16
Mortality: defined, 19; and Model A, 22-23; and Model B, 24; and Model C, 27; and selection, 27
Murray, S. L., viii, 17-31

N

NAACP Legal Defense and Educational Fund, 16
National Council of Measurement in Education (NCME), vii, 45, 47, 49
No-treatment expectation: equations for, 93; in Model A, 19, 93
Norm-referenced model. *See* Model A
Normal curve equivalent (NCE): as common metric, 7, 18, 34; conversion to, 24; gains in, 12-13
Normal growth, concept of, 12-13
Norwood, C. R., 21, 23, 25, 30

O

Office of Planning and Evaluation, 2, 13-14, 15
Office of Planning, Budgeting, and Evaluation (OPBE), 3-4
Office of Program Evaluation, 3, 11-12
Out-of-level testing: and cross-level referencing, 37-38; and equivalent scores, 38-40; problems with, 37-41; usefulness of, 57
Overall, J. E., 60, 82
Owens, T. R., 21, 22, 23, 25, 29
Ozenne, A., 21, 30

P

Pascal, A., 28
Pauly, E., 28
Pearson, K., 59, 62, 82
Pelavin, S. H., 3, 16, 21, 28, 39, 50, 56, 58
Pellegrini, 24, 26, 30
Peters, C. C., 74, 82
Pike, L. W., 43, 50
Ploden, R. E., 19, 28
Popham, W., 5, 15
Powell, G., 22, 23, 30, 31
Powers, S., 21, 23, 30
Preliminary Scholastic Aptitude Test (PSAT), 43–44
Price, G. G., 19, 28
Proctor, D. C., 21, 29
Public Law 93-380: Section 183 (f) of, 11; Section 183 (i) of, 10

R

Raffeld, P., viii, 22, 23, 30, 31, 55–58
Regression: additional theory of, 65–73; concepts of, 59–60; defined, 18; direct approach to, 85–88; and disattenuated correlation, 84–85; further, toward the mean, 78–80; history of theory on, 60–62; and Model A, 22; and Model B, 24; and Model C, 27; and negative correlations, 67–71; posttest versus pretest, on selection test, 84–88; and reliability coefficients, 65, 73–75; and selection, 25, 27; and test administration interval, 83–89; and truth and error composites, 62–64; to wrong mean, 75–78
Regression-effect bias, analysis of, 59–82
Regression model. See Model C
Reliability: of chance-level scores, 51–54; and functional-level testing, 35–36
Reliability coefficients: adjustments to, 73–75; inequality of, 65
Rhode Island, interlevel articulation in, 39
Rice, W., 23, 31
Rindler, S. E., 44, 49
Rivalry, compensatory: defined, 19; and Model C, 27
RMC Research Corporation, vii–viii, 3, 4, 8, 9, 10, 11, 18, 24, 34
Roberts, A. O. H., viii, 59–82, 83–86, 92–93, 95, 96

Roberts, O. A., 6, 11, 15, 20, 23, 30, 36, 50
Roberts, S. J., 31, 36, 37, 50, 75
Rogosa, D. R., 19, 28
Rosen, L., 4, 15
Rubin, D. B., 5, 7, 16, 44, 49

S

Sampling: changes in, 14; error of, and Model A, 21
Schaffran, J. A., 21, 30, 39, 50, 56, 58
Scherich, H., 21, 31
Schmid, J., 52, 54
Schmidt, J., 22, 23, 30
Scholastic Aptitude Test (SAT), 42–43
School and College Ability Tests (SCAT), 42
Seder, A., 38, 50
Selection: as bias source, 71, 92–93; defined, 18–19; effects of, and regression, 66; and Model A, 22; and Model B, 24–25; and Model C, 27; and posttest versus pretest regression, 84–88; and regression toward wrong mean, 75–78; and true score and error, 69–70
Selection, interaction with: defined, 19; and Model A, 23; and Model B, 25; and Model C, 27
Shoemaker, D., 14, 16
Slaughter, H. B., 21, 31
Slinde, J. A., 21, 31, 38–39, 40, 50
Smith, G., 86, 88
Smith, V. G., 29
Stammon, D., 22, 31
Stanford Research Institute, 3
Stanley, J. C., 19, 20, 24, 28, 42–43, 49
Statistical regression. See Regression
Stearnes, M., 23, 25, 30
Stenner, A. J., 13, 16, 22, 23, 31
Stewart, B. L., viii, 26, 31, 39–40, 41, 48, 50, 51–54
Stofflet, F. P., 21–22, 23, 25, 29
Storlie, T. R., 23, 31
Sustaining Effects Study, 8, 9, 12, 86
Systems Development Corporation, 9

T

Tallmadge, G. K., 3, 4, 5, 12, 13–14, 15, 16, 17, 21, 25, 31, 33, 50, 91, 96
TEMPO study, 3
Testing: defined, 18; and Model A, 20; and Model B, 24; and selection, 25, 27

Thistlethwaite, D. L., 19, 31

Thomas, T., 3, 16

Thorndike, R. L., 77, 82

Title I. *See* Elementary and Secondary Education Act

Title I Evaluation and Reporting System (TIERS): assumptions and biases of, 91–96; development of, vii–viii, 1–16; evolution of, 13–15; internal validity of, 17–31; and regression, 60

Title I Office, 2, 3

Tokar, E. B., 21–22, 23, 25, 29

Treatment: compensatory equalization of, 19, 27; diffusion or imitation of, 19, 23, 27

Treatment effect, nature of, 5, 17

U

U.S. Department of Education, 7

U.S. Department of Health, Education, and Welfare, 1

U.S. Office of Education (USOE), 5, 9, 10, 16, 59n

V

Vale, C. A., 38, 50

Validity: of chance-level scores, 51–54; classes of, 18; of TIERS, 17–31

Van Voorhis, W. R., 74, 82

W

Wang, M., 86, 88

Wargo, M., 3, 16

Washington Research Project, 3, 16

Weinfeld, F. D., 28

Williams, T., 21, 28

Wilson, K. M., viii, 33–50, 51, 54, 55–56

Winkler, R. L., 60, 82

Wisler, C., 4, 16

Womer, F. B., 52, 54

Wood, C. T., 3, 4, 5, 13–14, 15, 16, 17, 21, 22, 23, 25, 31, 33, 50, 91, 96

Woodward, J. A., 60, 82

Wright, B. D., 39, 50

Y

Yap, K. O., 22, 26, 31

York, R. L., 28

Yule, G. U., 60, 82

Z

Zellman, G., 28

New Directions Quarterly Sourcebooks

New Directions for Testing and Measurement is one of several distinct series of quarterly sourcebooks published by Jossey-Bass. The sourcebooks in each series are designed to serve both as *convenient compendiums* of the latest knowledge and practical experience on their topics and as *long-life reference tools*.

One-year, four-sourcebook subscriptions for each series cost $18 for individuals (when paid by personal check) and $30 for institutions, libraries, and agencies. Single copies of earlier sourcebooks are available at $6.95 each *prepaid* (or $7.95 each when *billed*).

A complete listing is given below of current and past sourcebooks in the *New Directions for Testing and Measurement* series. The titles and editors-in-chief of the other series are also listed. To subscribe, or to receive further information, write: New Directions Subscriptions, Jossey-Bass Inc., Publishers, 433 California Street, San Francisco, California 94104.

New Directions for Testing and Measurement
William B. Schrader, Editor-in-Chief
1979: 1. *Measurement and Educational Policy,*
          William B. Schrader
       2. *Insights from Large-Scale Surveys,* John Milholland
       3. *Impactive Changes on Measurement,* Roger Lennon
       4. *Methodological Developments,* Ross Traub
1980: 5. *Measuring Achievement: Progress Over a Decade,*
          William B. Schrader
       6. *Interpreting Test Performance,* Samuel T. Mayo
       7. *Recent Developments in Affective Measurement,*
          Samuel T. Mayo

New Directions for Child Development
William Damon, Editor-in-Chief

New Directions for College Learning Assistance
Kurt V. Lauridsen, Editor-in-Chief

New Directions for Community Colleges
Arthur M. Cohen, Editor-in-Chief
Florence B. Brawer, Associate Editor

New Directions for Continuing Education
Alan B. Knox, Editor-in-Chief